Live Holy and Godly Lives

The Books of 1 and 2 Peter

Dyron Daughrity

An Imprint of Sulis International Press
Los Angeles | Dallas | London

LIVE HOLY AND GODLY LIVES: THE BOOKS OF 1 AND 2 PETER
Copyright ©2024 by Dyron Daughrity. All rights reserved.

Except for brief quotations for reviews, no part of this book may be reproduced in any form or by any electronic or mechanical means, including information storage and retrieval systems, without written permission from the publisher. Email: info@sulisinternational.com.

Cover photo by Noah Silliman on Unsplash
Cover design by Sulis International Press.

ISBN (print): 978-1-958139-47-9
ISBN (eBook): 978-1-958139-48-6

Published by Keledei Publications
An Imprint of Sulis International
Los Angeles | Dallas | London

www.sulisinternational.com

Contents

1. You Are Peter (Part 1) 1
2. You are Peter (Part 2) 15
3. Holy Foreigners (1 Peter 1) 31
4. Speak Honorably (1 Peter 2) 41
5. The Functional Marriage (1 Peter 3) 51
6. The Eyes, Ears, and Face of God (1 Peter 3) 63
7. This Water Symbolizes Baptism (1 Peter 3:18 – 4:11) 73
8. How to Suffer Well (1 Peter 4:12-19) 83
9. Respect for Elders (1 Peter 5:1-6) 93
10. Confirm Your Calling (2 Peter 1:1-11) 103
11. Remember These Things (2 Peter 1:12-21) 113
12. Watch out for False Teachers (2 Peter 2) 123
13. The Last Days (2 Peter 3) 135

1. You Are Peter (Part 1)

There are many elements that compose a person's identity. Diving into the identity of Peter, we are drawn towards his name. The name "Peter" comes from the Greek word for "rock," or, "petros." However, Jesus and the apostles often referred to him by his given name, "Kephas," which is the Aramaic word for "rock." Aramaic was the mother tongue to Jesus and the apostles; it was the language they spoke to one another and to their families. Today, we've anglicized the name "Kephas" to "Cephas" (See-fuss). A third name for Peter is "Simon," as in "Simon Peter." In Greek, this name is "Symeon." In Hebrew, it is "Shimone."

Peter was a Jew, and he was from the Galilean town of Bethsaida. The geography of Israel was based around *five bodies of water*. To the west was the Mediterranean Sea. Way down in the south is the Red Sea. On the east of Israel is the extremely salty Dead Sea—the lowest body of water in the world. And up in the north of Israel is the freshwater "Sea of Galilee," which is actually the world's lowest *freshwater* lake. The first 3 bodies of water are often known as the Med, the Red, and the Dead. The majority of Israel's drinking water is from the Sea of Galilee—which is where Jesus and his apostles are from. The fifth and final body of water is the

Jordan River that runs from Mount Hermon—in Lebanon—flows south, and empties into the Dead Sea.

In the summer of 2022, Archeologists found the home of the apostle Peter in Bethsaida. There was an ancient Greek inscription that read, "The chief and commander of the heavenly apostles." There was a Byzantine basilica built over it. The floor was several layers deep, and many coins and pottery pieces dating to the first century were unearthed there.

Peter likely grew up in this house, in this village, near the Sea of Galilee, in first century Israel. At some point, he married a woman (Mark 1:30) who joined him on missionary journeys (1 Cor. 9:5). Peter was a fisherman, which was a fitting analogy for Jesus to use whenever he urged his new disciples to switch from being fishermen to "fishers of men" (Mark 1:17).

It must have been a major decision for Peter and his brother, Andrew, to stop their livelihood of fishing and —just like that—start following this powerful, prophetic teacher who could literally heal people of disease and physical abnormalities.

Andrew actually introduced him to Jesus. Both Peter and Andrew had been disciples of John the Baptist (John 1:40-42), but then met Jesus.

Peter plays a prominent place in the New Testament, as he was one of the 12 apostles. It is clear from the gospels that Jesus's closest friends were Peter, James, and John. The brothers James and John were often known as "the sons of Zebedee."

The Gospel of Mark is thought by scholars to represent Peter's perspective. It is probably the earliest of the gospels. It has a pithy, fast-paced narrative, and is the shortest gospel. It has an early, raw feel to it, with less finesse than the other three gospels.

You should know that whenever the New Testament writers list the apostles, they usually put Peter's name first (Mk. 3:16, Acts 1:13).

And Peter is associated with some of the most memorable scenes in the gospels, but not all of these texts are favorable towards him. They show us that Jesus used a flawed person to spread His message in the earliest day of His ministry. Here is Mark 8:27-37, a good introduction to Peter's strengths and weaknesses:

> *Jesus and his disciples went on to the villages around Caesarea Philippi. On the way, he asked them, "Who do people say I am?"*
>
> *They replied, "Some say John the Baptist; others say Elijah; and still others, one of the prophets."*
>
> *"But what about you?" he asked. "Who do you say I am?"*
>
> *Peter answered, "You are the Messiah."*
>
> *Jesus warned them not to tell anyone about him.*
>
> *He then began to teach them that the Son of Man must suffer many things and be rejected by the elders, the chief priests and the teachers*

of the law, and that he must be killed, and after three days rise again. He spoke plainly about this, and Peter took him aside and began to rebuke him.

But when Jesus turned and looked at his disciples, he rebuked Peter. "Get behind me, Satan!" he said. "You do not have in mind the concerns of God, but merely human concerns."

Then he called the crowd to him along with his disciples and said: "Whoever wants to be my disciple must deny themselves and take up their cross and follow me. For whoever wants to save their life will lose it, but whoever loses their life for me and for the gospel will save it. What good is it for someone to gain the whole world, yet forfeit their soul? Or what can anyone give in exchange for their soul? If anyone is ashamed of me and my words in this adulterous and sinful generation, the Son of Man will be ashamed of them when he comes in his Father's glory with the holy angels."

This passage has so much in it. You see Peter's desire to protect Jesus, but Jesus making it clear he did not need protecting. He needed following. And Peter needed to accept that both Jesus and Peter himself would have to suffer for the Kingdom of God, for the sake of Jesus.

Another classic text showing Peter's excitable personality is that famous text called "The Transfiguration" in Mark 9:2-10:

After six days, Jesus took Peter, James and John with him and led them up a high mountain, where they were all alone. There he was transfigured before them. His clothes became dazzling white, whiter than anyone in the world could bleach them. And there appeared before them Elijah and Moses, who were talking with Jesus.

Peter said to Jesus, "Rabbi, it is good for us to be here. Let us put up three shelters—one for you, one for Moses and one for Elijah." (He did not know what to say, they were so frightened.)

Then a cloud appeared and covered them, and a voice came from the cloud: "This is my Son, whom I love. Listen to him!"

Suddenly, when they looked around, they no longer saw anyone with them except Jesus.

As they were coming down the mountain, Jesus gave them orders not to tell anyone what they had seen until the Son of Man had risen from the dead. They kept the matter to themselves, discussing what "rising from the dead" meant.

In Mark 14:32-37, we see Peter letting Jesus down again when he fell asleep while Jesus wanted him to stay awake and pray. This was in the Garden of Gethsemane, the night before Jesus's crucifixion.

> *They went to a place called Gethsemane, and Jesus said to his disciples, "Sit here while I pray." He took Peter, James and John along with him, and he began to be deeply distressed and troubled. "My soul is overwhelmed with sorrow to the point of death," he said to them. "Stay here and keep watch."*
>
> *Going a little farther, he fell to the ground and prayed that if possible the hour might pass from him. "Abba, Father," he said, "everything is possible for you. Take this cup from me. Yet not what I will, but what you will."*
>
> *Then he returned to his disciples and found them sleeping. "Simon," he said to Peter, "are you asleep? Couldn't you keep watch for one hour? Watch and pray so that you will not fall into temptation. The spirit is willing, but the flesh is weak."*

And then, most memorable of all, we encounter the great act of betrayal, committed by Peter, just as Jesus was getting arrested. This fascinating text is in Mark 14:66-72:

> *While Peter was below in the courtyard, one of the servant girls of the high priest came by. When she saw Peter warming himself, she*

looked closely at him. "You also were with that Nazarene, Jesus," she said.

But he denied it. "I don't know or understand what you're talking about," he said, and went out into the entryway. When the servant girl saw him there, she said again to those standing around, "This fellow is one of them." Again, he denied it. After a little while, those standing near said to Peter, "Surely you are one of them, for you are a Galilean." He began to call down curses, and he swore to them, "I don't know this man you're talking about."

Immediately, the rooster crowed the second time. Then Peter remembered the word Jesus had spoken to him: "Before the rooster crows twice you will disown me three times." And he broke down and wept.

Scholars tell us that by cursing Jesus and completely disowning him, Peter removed himself from the ranks of the apostles. As proof of this idea, we see this interesting passage that took place right after Jesus was risen. In Mark 16:4-7:

But when they looked up, they saw that the stone, which was very large, had been rolled away. As they entered the tomb, they saw a young man dressed in a white robe sitting on the right side, and they were alarmed.

> *"Don't be alarmed," he said. "You are looking for Jesus the Nazarene, who was crucified. He has risen! He is not here. See the place where they laid him. But go, tell his disciples and Peter, 'He is going ahead of you into Galilee. There you will see him, just as he told you.'"*

Did you catch that? "Tell his disciples and Peter." No longer is Peter part of the disciples. He broke the cardinal rule—he denied Jesus. He denied the Lord. He severed himself from Christ. It was a case of blasphemy, coming from the apostle that Jesus referred to as "the rock." Peter was solid. But all of that rock-hard commitment fell away when Peter was tested.

Remember, there was a time when Jesus saw so much potential in Peter. Listen to these words that Jesus said to Peter, in Matthew 16:15-20:

> *"But what about you?" he asked. "Who do you say I am?"*
>
> *Simon Peter answered, "You are the Messiah, the Son of the living God."*
>
> *Jesus replied, "Blessed are you, Simon son of Jonah, for this was not revealed to you by flesh and blood, but by my Father in heaven. And I tell you that you are Peter, and on this rock I will build my church, and the gates of Hades will not overcome it. I will give you the keys of the kingdom of heaven; whatever you bind on*

> *earth will be bound in heaven, and whatever*
> *you loose on earth will be loosed in heaven."*
> *Then he ordered his disciples not to tell anyone*
> *that he was the Messiah.*

Jesus must have been devastated when this "rock" of a disciple abandoned Him, and denied Him. Peter knew better. He had faithfully followed Jesus for three years. Remember, Peter was the one who jumped out of the boat and ran on the water to embrace Jesus, who was walking on the water in the middle of a storm.

Peter was the enthusiastic disciple who was ready to fight for Jesus in the Garden of Gethsemane in John 18:4-11:

> *Jesus, knowing all that was going to happen to*
> *him, went out and asked them, "Who is it you*
> *want?"*
>
> *"Jesus of Nazareth," they replied.*
>
> *"I am he," Jesus said. (And Judas the traitor*
> *was standing there with them.) When Jesus*
> *said, "I am he," they drew back and fell to the*
> *ground.*
>
> *Again he asked them, "Who is it you want?"*
>
> *"Jesus of Nazareth," they said.*
>
> *Jesus answered, "I told you that I am he. If*
> *you are looking for me, then let these men go."*
> *This happened so that the words he had spoken*

would be fulfilled: "I have not lost one of those you gave me."

Then Simon Peter, who had a sword, drew it and struck the high priest's servant, cutting off his right ear. (The servant's name was Malchus.)

Jesus commanded Peter, "Put your sword away! Shall I not drink the cup the Father has given me?"

According to the gospels, Jesus knew that Peter had weaknesses. His faith was not firm. Jesus knew Peter was strong, but he also knew that Peter was a man, and he had fears and frailties like all of us. In fact, Jesus knew that Peter was going to deny Him even before it even happened. We read this in Luke 22:31-34:

"Simon, Simon, Satan has asked to sift all of you as wheat. But I have prayed for you, Simon, that your faith may not fail. And when you have turned back, strengthen your brothers."

But he replied, "Lord, I am ready to go with you to prison and to death."

Jesus answered, "I tell you, Peter, before the rooster crows today, you will deny three times that you know me."

We all know that Peter denied Jesus three times. However, Jesus did not leave Peter there to drown in his guilt and shame. Rather, Jesus restored Peter to the ministry with this wonderful little story in John 21:12-19:

> *Jesus said to them, "Come and have breakfast." None of the disciples dared ask him, "Who are you?" They knew it was the Lord. Jesus came, took the bread and gave it to them, and did the same with the fish. This was now the third time Jesus appeared to his disciples after he was raised from the dead.*
>
> *When they had finished eating, Jesus said to Simon Peter, "Simon son of John, do you love me more than these?"*
>
> *"Yes, Lord," he said, "you know that I love you."*
>
> *Jesus said, "Feed my lambs."*
>
> *Again, Jesus said, "Simon son of John, do you love me?"*
>
> *He answered, "Yes, Lord, you know that I love you."*
>
> *Jesus said, "Take care of my sheep."*
>
> *The third time he said to him, "Simon son of John, do you love me?"*

> *Peter was hurt because Jesus asked him the third time, "Do you love me?" He said, "Lord, you know all things; you know that I love you."*
>
> *Jesus said, "Feed my sheep. Very truly I tell you, when you were younger, you dressed yourself and went where you wanted; but when you are old you will stretch out your hands, and someone else will dress you and lead you where you do not want to go." Jesus said this to indicate the kind of death by which Peter would glorify God. Then he said to him, "Follow me!"*

Something that scholars have clued into in recent years is that by Jesus questioning Peter three times, he was offering him redemption for the three denials. It is beautiful the way Jesus did this.

However, Jesus also promises Peter something else. He promises him that he will die a martyr. And Peter did, during the persecution of Christians by the Roman Emperor Nero.

But that's getting ahead of ourselves. In the next chapter, we'll unpack Peter's apostolic career, after the gospel texts. We'll also connect Peter's life to his two New Testament letters, 1 and 2 Peter.

So, what are the take-homes for this chapter? Here they are:

1. Peter was imperfect, but Jesus still loved him deeply, and called Him to do great work for God.

2. You are imperfect, but Jesus still loves you deeply, and calls you to do great work for God.

Now let's talk about you and me. Maybe you think you've really messed up, and you are not worthy of Jesus's love. Or you feel like you've done something so shameful that you can't let it go.

Well, let me assure you. You've probably not reached the level that Peter did—outright denying Jesus three times, cursing against the Lord, and completely turning your back on Him.

Peter did that. Yes, Peter did pretty much the worst thing a person can do—completely turn against the Lord—to the point of denying that he ever even knew Jesus.

But our God is a god of forgiveness. You can turn back to Jesus, and he will forgive you. And then he will simply utter those familiar words that He did to Peter: "Follow me."

You screwed up. You let yourself down. Maybe you feel you let the Lord down. It's okay. Your sins are forgiven if you truly are repentant. Now it's time to turn back to Jesus. And he says those two words that cut through all of the complications of our past failures: "Follow me." Get up off the floor. Pull up your sleeves and get back to work.

2. You are Peter (Part 2)

In the last chapter, we looked at most of the main stories from the Gospels that feature Peter. He was one of Jesus' closest friends. Whenever Jesus went off with just a few chosen apostles, he nearly always chose Peter, James, and John. Peter and Jesus had a very close relationship. We know that Peter disowned Jesus when Jesus was about to be crucified. Remember, he did that three times before the rooster crowed in the morning. But, in the end, Jesus forgave Peter by "reinstating him" with the words, "Do you love me? Then feed my sheep."

Jesus forgave Peter, and then commanded him, "Follow me."

Peter emerges from that powerful experience—of denying Jesus and then being forgiven by Jesus—as a very different man. No longer is Peter the weak-willed one. No longer is he the one who hedges. No longer is he the one who acts like a big defender of Jesus one moment, yet resolutely denies Jesus the next moment.

The repentant and forgiven Peter is a different Peter. So, let's talk about that Peter as we look at his life after the closing of the gospels—Matthew, Mark, Luke, and John.

In the book of Acts, Peter emerges as the leader of the apostles. It is a striking change. The book of Acts is crucial to understanding Peter's transformation into a bold and unequivocal leader. The book of Acts is somewhat divided between chapters 1-12, and then 13 through 28 (the last chapter). The first 12 chapters tend to focus a lot on Peter. And chapters 13-28 tend to focus on the ministry of Paul.

In Acts 1:14–15, we see Peter clearly taking a leadership role among the apostles while gathered at the Mount of Olives. We are told the eleven apostles are there (as Judas committed suicide out of shame for betraying Jesus). They are joined by Mary, the mother of Jesus, along with some of the "women" and "Jesus's brothers." There were others there as well. Luke—the author of Acts—tells us that there were around 120 people gathered. Luke tells us that they were "joining constantly in prayer."

That's when Peter stands up and mentions the fact that Judas committed suicide, and thus they needed to replace him to keep the number of apostles at twelve. So, they chose a man named Matthias.

Then in Acts 2 we get the famous scene where the Holy Spirit comes at the Pentecost gathering in Jerusalem. There's wind, and something they described as "tongues of fire" resting on everyone, and the apostles speaking in other languages. Onlookers actually accused the apostles of being drunk, "They have had too much wine." (Acts 2:13)

Then, for a second time, Peter stands up among the other apostles. And he gives a sermon, based on a prophecy in the Old Testament book of Joel. That sermon is often called the first gospel sermon. Here are some important excerpts from that sermon (Acts 2:21-24; 32, 36–41):

Everyone who calls on the name of the Lord will be saved.

Fellow Israelites, listen to this: Jesus of Nazareth was a man accredited by God to you by miracles, wonders and signs, which God did among you through him, as you yourselves know. This man was handed over to you by God's deliberate plan and foreknowledge; and you, with the help of wicked men, put him to death by nailing him to the cross. But God raised him from the dead, freeing him from the agony of death, because it was impossible for death to keep its hold on him.

God has raised this Jesus to life, and we are all witnesses of it. Exalted to the right hand of God, he has received from the Father the promised Holy Spirit and has poured out what you now see and hear.

Therefore, let all Israel be assured of this: God has made this Jesus, whom you crucified, both Lord and Messiah.

> *When the people heard this, they were cut to the heart and said to Peter and the other apostles, "Brothers, what shall we do?"*
>
> *Peter replied, "Repent and be baptized, every one of you, in the name of Jesus Christ for the forgiveness of your sins. And you will receive the gift of the Holy Spirit. The promise is for you and your children and for all who are far off—for all whom the Lord our God will call."*
>
> *With many other words he warned them; and he pleaded with them, "Save yourselves from this corrupt generation." Those who accepted his message were baptized, and about three thousand were added to their number that day.*

And there you have it ... the first post-resurrection gospel sermon. It is very clear and to the point. And it tells us, very succinctly, the core of the Christian message—and how we, personally, are to respond. Peter makes it clear, we are to "Repent and be baptized, in the name of Jesus Christ, for the forgiveness of sins, and you will receive the gift of the Holy Spirit." Peter says it is a promise. And it is for all.

In Acts 3, we see the power of the Holy Spirit working miraculously in Peter's ministry. He heals a man who couldn't walk. The man was begging for money, but Peter uttered those famous words in Acts 3:6,

> *"Silver or gold I do not have, but what I do have I give you. In the name of Jesus Christ of Nazareth, walk."*

The text says Peter took the man by the hand, helped him up, and instantly the man was healed. He began to walk, and even started to jump while praising God. Interested, a big crowd of people gathered around to witness what was happening, and that's when Peter launched into another sermon, in Acts 3:11-16:

> *"Fellow Israelites, why does this surprise you? Why do you stare at us as if by our own power or godliness we had made this man walk? The God of Abraham, Isaac and Jacob, the God of our fathers, has glorified his servant Jesus. You handed him over to be killed, and you disowned him before Pilate, though he had decided to let him go. You disowned the Holy and Righteous One and asked that a murderer be released to you. You killed the author of life, but God raised him from the dead. We are witnesses of this. By faith in the name of Jesus, this man whom you see and know was made strong. It is Jesus' name and the faith that comes through him that has completely healed him, as you can all see."*

One thing you'll notice when reading about Peter's ministry is that he is extremely familiar with the Old Testament. In that passage in Acts 3, he mentions Moses, Samuel, and Abraham. Peter became one of the great apostles to the Jews, whereas Paul became the great apostle to the Gentiles. They both knew the Old Testament text backwards and forwards, but Peter had a special heart for his people, the Jews.

In Acts 4, we see just how far Peter had come. He was now a bold follower of Jesus, and a faithful and courageous preacher. We're told that Peter and John were preaching about the resurrection of Jesus when they were arrested and put into jail. This arrest didn't stop their ministry, though. In Acts 4:3-4,

The priests and the captain of the temple guard and the Sadducees came up to Peter and John while they were speaking to the people. They were greatly disturbed because the apostles were teaching the people, proclaiming in Jesus the resurrection of the dead. They seized Peter and John and, because it was evening, they put them in jail until the next day. But many who heard the message believed; so the number of men who believed grew to about five thousand.

Did you catch that? The number of men had reached 5,000, but when you add the women and children, we might be talking ten to fifteen thousand followers of Jesus.

So Peter and John get arrested, but then Peter, it says, "filled with the Holy Spirit," said this (Acts 4:9-12):

If we are being called to account today for an act of kindness shown to a man who was lame and are being asked how he was healed, then know this, you and all the people of Israel: It is by the name of Jesus Christ of Nazareth, whom

you crucified but whom God raised from the dead, that this man stands before you healed. Jesus is the stone you builders rejected, which has become the cornerstone. Salvation is found in no one else, for there is no other name under heaven given to mankind by which we must be saved.

So how did the rulers and elders respond to Peter? Pay attention to this fascinating text, found in Acts 4:13-22:

When they saw the courage of Peter and John and realized that they were unschooled, ordinary men, they were astonished and they took note that these men had been with Jesus. But since they could see the man who had been healed standing there with them, there was nothing they could say. So they ordered them to withdraw from the Sanhedrin and then conferred together. "What are we going to do with these men?" they asked. "Everyone living in Jerusalem knows they have performed a notable sign, and we cannot deny it. But to stop this thing from spreading any further among the people, we must warn them to speak no longer to anyone in this name."

Then they called them in again and commanded them not to speak or teach at all in the name of Jesus. But Peter and John replied, "Which is right in God's eyes: to listen to you, or to him? You be the judges! As for us, we cannot help speaking about what we have seen and heard."

After further threats, they let them go. They could not decide how to punish them, because all the people were praising God for what had happened. For the man who was miraculously healed was over forty years old.

Clearly, Peter was not going to stop talking about Jesus. He did not fear men anymore, as he had weeks prior. Peter was a new man.

Next, we see Peter confronting a man and wife named Ananias and Sapphira, as they were among the early Christians. This was at a time when people were giving to the Lord in order to support the work of the church. This couple—Ananias and Sapphira—claimed they were giving the apostles the proceeds of the sale of a piece of their land. However, they lied about how much they earned in the sale. Peter confronted them about it, and they both lied about it. Shortly after their lies, both of them died. It caused great fear in the early community, and it was a lesson in why we must be honest both with God and with our fellow brothers and sisters in Christ.

Peter's reputation grew among the early Christians, largely because they began to see him as a person who could heal them. Read this passage, from Acts 5:14–16:

More and more men and women believed in the Lord and were added to their number. As a result, people brought the sick into the streets and laid them on beds and mats so that at least Peter's shadow might fall on some of them as he passed by. Crowds gathered also from the towns around Jerusalem, bringing their sick and those tormented by impure spirits, and all of them were healed.

Then Peter gets jailed again, and—again—they tell him not to talk about Jesus anymore. And the book of Acts tells us how Peter and the others responded to these demands, in Acts 5:27–31.

The apostles were brought in and made to appear before the Sanhedrin to be questioned by the high priest. "We gave you strict orders not to teach in this name," he said. "Yet you have filled Jerusalem with your teaching and are determined to make us guilty of this man's blood."

Peter and the other apostles replied: "We must obey God rather than human beings! The God of our ancestors raised Jesus from the dead—whom you killed by hanging him on a cross. God exalted him to his own right hand as Prince and Savior, that he might bring Israel to repentance and forgive their sins."

And so how did the religious leaders respond to Peter's speech? The Bible tells us that they had Peter and the apostles flogged. Here is what it says in Acts 5:40b–42:

They called the apostles in and had them flogged. Then they ordered them not to speak in the name of Jesus, and let them go.

The apostles left the Sanhedrin, *rejoicing* because they had been counted worthy of suffering disgrace for the Name. Day after day, in the temple courts and from house to house, they never stopped teaching and proclaiming the good news that Jesus is the Messiah.

I think it is really amazing that when they were ordered to not preach the gospel, Peter and the others simply continued to obey God, and not the human authorities.

In Acts 10, we encounter an important story that is too long to recount here, and it has to do with God choosing Peter to spread the gospel to the Gentiles. It all began when an Italian solder named Cornelius had a vision. In the vision, Cornelius is commanded to send for Peter.

Around the same time, Peter, too, had a vision. It was of a large sheet being let down to earth, and containing all kinds of animals that Jews were not to eat. Then a voice said to Peter, "Get up, Peter. Kill and eat."

But Peter was a faithful Jew, so he protested, "I have never eaten anything impure or unclean!"

Then the voice said, "Do not call anything impure that God has made clean."

So, next, Peter goes to Cornelius's house, still wondering about that vision. However, after a time, Peter came to this conclusion, in Acts 10:28:

> *He said to them: "You are well aware that it is against our law for a Jew to associate with or visit a Gentile. But God has shown me that I should not call anyone impure or unclean."*

And that was a major moment in the history of Christianity. It was at that moment that it became clear that Christianity was not just for Jews. It was for all people. Peter was a key figure in that important shift. And in that same chapter, we see Gentiles get baptized into Christ. It was pivotal!

The final time we encounter Peter in the book of Acts is at the famous Council of Jerusalem, which happened in A.D. 50. You get all the big guns there: Peter, Barnabas, Paul, and James (the brother of Jesus). At that gathering, these four men spoke and gave their famous conclusion in Acts 15:5-20, that Gentiles could join the new Christian faith (I'm having to condense a bit here):

Then some of the believers who belonged to the party of the Pharisees stood up and said, "The Gentiles must be circumcised and required to keep the law of Moses."

The apostles and elders met to consider this question. After much discussion, Peter got up and addressed them:

> *Brothers, you know that some time ago God made a choice among you that the Gentiles might hear from my lips the message of the gospel and believe. God, who knows the heart, showed that he accepted them by giving the Holy Spirit to them, just as he did to us. He did not discriminate between us and them, for he purified their hearts by faith. Now then, why do you try to test God by putting on the necks of Gentiles a yoke that neither we nor our ancestors have been able to bear? No! We believe it is through the grace of our Lord Jesus that we are saved, just as they are.*

The whole assembly became silent as they listened to Barnabas and Paul telling about the signs and wonders

God had done among the Gentiles through them. When they finished, James spoke up.

> *"Brothers," he said, "listen to me. Simon has described to us how God first intervened to choose a people for his name from the Gentiles. It is my judgment, therefore, that we should not make it difficult for the Gentiles who are turning to God."*

Peter and Paul had won the day. However, that's not the end of the story. In Paul's epistle to the Galatians, we read of a fascinating little incident where Paul tells us that Peter backslid into error on this issue. Peter started backing away from the Gentiles. And Paul was livid about. Let's read this text, in Galatians 2:9–16.

> *James, Cephas, and John, those esteemed as pillars, gave me and Barnabas the right hand of fellowship when they recognized the grace given to me. They agreed that we should go to the Gentiles, and they to the circumcised. All they asked was that we should continue to remember the poor, the very thing I had been eager to do all along.*
>
> *When Cephas [Peter] came to Antioch, I opposed him to his face, because he stood condemned. For before certain men came from James, he used to eat with the Gentiles. But when they arrived, he began to draw back and separate himself from the Gentiles because he*

> *was afraid of those who belonged to the circumcision group. The other Jews joined him in his hypocrisy, so that by their hypocrisy even Barnabas was led astray.*
>
> *When I saw that they were not acting in line with the truth of the gospel, I said to Cephas (Peter) in front of them all, "You are a Jew, yet you live like a Gentile and not like a Jew. How is it, then, that you force Gentiles to follow Jewish customs?"*
>
> *"We who are Jews by birth and not sinful Gentiles know that a person is not justified by the works of the law, but by faith in Jesus Christ. So, we, too, have put our faith in Christ Jesus that we may be justified by faith in Christ and not by the works of the law, because by the works of the law no one will be justified."*

So, we see that even great men of God can backslide. They can quarrel. But in this case, Paul corrected Peter. And, we can presume that Peter accepted the correction, because Peter was absolutely wrong in this case. And Peter knew it. He had "drawn back" away from the Gentiles because in the ultra-Jewish mind, Gentiles were unclean.

We can assume that Peter pulled himself together and stopped this avoidance of the Gentiles. Peter knew better.

That's pretty much the end of the historical record for Peter. Later in his ministry he wrote 1 and 2 Peter. After that, we simply don't know much about what happened to him. The historical record gets pretty fuzzy.

In Galatians, Paul's confrontation with Peter is in the city of Antioch. This was an important church. It was the place where the early believers were first called "Christians." The Antiochian church also supported Paul's missionary journeys. We know Peter was living there for a while.

Some claim Peter later went to Rome, although this has never been proven. Others claim Peter was killed in the persecution under Emperor Nero, which is very likely. One important church tradition says that Peter was crucified, but when it came time to crucify him, he begged them to crucify him upside down—saying he was not worthy to be crucified in the same way as his Lord.

What are the main takeaways from this chapter? Here are three:

1. People can change. Peter vacillated at one point in his life. But by the end, he was steadfast and committed. Some of you have changed in the course of your life. You were lost, and then you became found. Praise God that we can change.

2. Our faith is anchored in Judaism. But Peter and Paul remind us that Jesus is for everyone. Yes, he was Jewish, but he died for the sins of all mankind. Including you and me.

3. God calls people to service in His kingdom. God called Peter. God called Paul. But God also calls

you. And He calls me. And if we want the Gospel to continue to spread ... then we must give Him our lives. Peter and Paul are gone. It is now our turn to spread the message.

3. Holy Foreigners (1 Peter 1)

We will be studying the "Petrine Epistles" over the next several chapters. What do we mean by "Petrine Epistles?" These are the Epistles of Peter, in other words, 1 and 2 Peter. Both of these letters are found near the end of your Bible. I want to encourage you to get familiar with these two little documents in the New Testament.

The letter of First Peter is excellent, especially for new Christians and those who are realizing how different the Christian life is, as opposed to a worldly life.

The book of First Peter had a huge influence on me when I was truly starting to give my life to Christ, back when I was around 19 or 20 years old. First Peter is about how to live as a Christian in this troubled world. As Jesus said in John 15:19, "… You do not belong to the world, but I have chosen you out of the world. That is why the world hates you."

That is an important idea right there, coming right out of the mouth of the Lord. We do not belong to this world. Like Jesus, our true home is in heaven, in God's kingdom. And this might get us into trouble sometimes, just as it did the early Christians.

You see, friends, the early Christians—our ancestors in the faith—they were often persecuted. They were despised and rejected, much like Jesus was. As we all know, Jesus was so despised and rejected that they crucified him. The mob surrounded him and arrested him. They made fun of him and jeered at him. They inflicted indescribable violence onto him.

And the early followers of Jesus realized that they, too, could eventually get "found out" for being a secret follower of Jesus. The early Christians had to meet in catacombs under the ground to worship. They had to move around to other cities sometimes in order to keep themselves from being found out. They met in secret so as not to invite persecution upon themselves and their loved ones.

History shows that the early Christians were badly mistreated. Christianity was illegal from the time of the apostles all the way to the early 300s!

Some of the early Christians were beaten. Some were burned. Some were placed into a Roman arena to be killed by wild animals. Many Christians were called out, defamed publicly, paraded in the streets, and tortured. Much like Jesus. In fact, the author of 1 and 2 Peter was the apostle Peter, who was killed for his faith in Christ. These were all part of being a Christian in the first, second, third, and early fourth century.

So in this book, I want to take you back to the context of early Christianity. First Peter was written to provide comfort for a suffering people. It is full of helpful advice on how to manage being a Christian in a world that punishes you for being a Christian.

Let us look at First Peter 1:6-9:

6 In all this you greatly rejoice, though now for a little while you may have had to suffer grief in all kinds of trials. 7 These have come so that the proven genuineness of your faith—of greater worth than gold, which perishes even though refined by fire—may result in praise, glory and honor when Jesus Christ is revealed. 8 Though you have not seen him, you love him; and even though you do not see him now, you believe in him and are filled with an inexpressible and glorious joy, 9 for you are receiving the end result of your faith, the salvation of your souls.

Some of us have had to suffer some grief in life. I got to thinking this week: I totally enjoy those times when I get to play around with my 9-year-old, Holly Joy. I often think to myself how innocent she is. Life is so happy for her. She laughs and plays, and has no worries. And that is as it should be. She often kisses me on both of my cheeks before she heads to bed. She has no cares in the world, other than playing, giving love to Sunde and me, and getting into the occasional spat with her siblings. But she has a life that is pretty much worry free. Imagine that ... A life that is completely worry free.

Boy, it is very different when you are all grown up ... in my case 50 years old. Life inevitably gives you some weary days. Life will grind many of us down over the years. You see this with American presidents. They go into office all eager and full of optimism. They leave, looking 20 years older.

Some of you have had to deal with really heavy burdens: a broken marriage, bankruptcy, a falling out with your best friend, poverty, the sudden loss of employment, cancer, betrayal by a lover, rejection from a parent, a broken hip, surgeries, disease, eye problems. *The list just gets longer the older we get!*

But Peter reminds us that suffering has been going on among God's people since day one. Christianity was never intended to be a faith aimed at earthly success. Our greatest rewards are awaiting us in heaven. There is always pain and difficulty when we follow Jesus ... and when we turn our backs on the mobs, the herds of people, the large and paved roads. Jesus tells us that the road is narrow that leads to salvation. It is a difficult path, where you have to bear a cross. You will have wind in your face. You will "suffer grief in all kinds of trials" as Peter says in verse 6.

The good news, however, is that your faith is proved genuine during these times of suffering. Peter uses the analogy of gold. You have to burn gold using very high temperatures in order to burn out all of the impurities. Similarly, you and I will have to suffer the purifying process. We will have to go through these trials. We will have to be "refined by fire."

Oddly enough, Peter tells us that we can still find joy amidst these trials, and amidst the refining process. We are moving closer to salvation. If tested and proven worthy, we will receive the "end result of our faith: the salvation of our souls" (v. 9).

It is important to remember this: you need to be joyful deep down, even during difficult days. God sees you. You are not suffering for nothing. You don't have pain for nothing. No, God is refining you. God is making you holy. He is getting the bad stuff out of you so you can shine like gold.

In chapter 1: 13-16, we get this from the apostle Peter:

> *13 Therefore, with minds that are alert and fully sober, set your hope on the grace to be brought to you when Jesus Christ is revealed at his coming. 14 As obedient children, do not conform to the evil desires you had when you lived in ignorance. 15 But just as he who called you is holy, so be holy in all you do; 16 for it is written: "Be holy, because I am holy."*

What this text is saying is you need to remain alert and sober. Don't drown your sorrows in alcohol, or try to escape mentally. Rather, keep your hope. Hope in the Lord. Know that Jesus is coming back one day, and he will be looking for his faithful ones. Don't "conform" to the evil desires that sinners succumb to. Live above all of that nonsense. Don't sink into a sinful state of mind when you get discouraged. Rather, keep the faith. "Be holy," Peter says, "because God is holy."

We should strive to live like the example that Jesus set for us. We are God's children. We know who we are. That's our identity. Let's choose to live holy lives, and honor God with our conduct. So many people are struggling with identity these days. They don't know who they are. But Christians don't have an identity crisis. We know where our loyalties lie. Our loyalty lies with Jesus Christ. We love him. And we reject the compromising temptations that this world places before us. We refuse to lower our standards like that.

In First Peter 1:17, we read this: 17 Since you call on a Father who judges each person's work impartially, live out your time as foreigners here in reverent fear.

1 Peter 1:21 says, "... your faith and hope are in God."

The title of this chapter is "Holy Foreigners," because that is what we are supposed to be. This world is not our home. We are foreigners. We live here, but this is not the most comfortable place for us. Our "home" is with our sisters and brothers in heaven. What a day that will be when we walk into heaven and see our loved ones, and see Jesus, and witness the most beautiful worship we've ever witnessed before.

We will finally be able to stand before God, our creator. I wonder what he will be like. I don't think God will be in the form of a man. I think God will be something grander than anything we can imagine right now. I think the music will be exhilarating. I think the people there will be so kind, so pure, so encouraging. I think there will be peace in heaven that will make us so calm and contented. We will feel "whole"—a concept the Jews call "Shalom."

Heaven will be a place where you and I will feel so accepted. We will finally feel *understood*. We will feel forgiven, truly forgiven, for our sins, and the mistakes we made. There will be no shame or guilt. No one will curse. No one will be sad. It will be a *perfected* world.

In the meantime, however, we are in a place of much suffering. Now, maybe your life is great, like Holly Joy's. I hope so. Maybe you think to yourself that life is relatively easy, without too many trials. If that's your life, then let me be the first to congratulate you. But most lives on earth are not like that. It's not like we're running around trying to escape the sword of the Roman soldiers.

But, to be honest, sometimes it feels like life is a long journey, punctuated by loss, fear, anxiety, broken relationships, and sometimes *real* pain. Just this past weekend, my wife's grandmother passed away. So did my best friend's dad, as well as my mentor's dad. And a woman in our church lost a close friend. All of these individuals passed away during the holidays; right around Christmas.

I have traveled much to India, where I see children whose parents are nowhere to be found. I see people who live in slums, next to the city dump, so they can pick through the heaps of trash for items to keep.

But even here, in the United States. There is real pain. There are real challenges. For instance, Sunde, my wife, grew up without a dad. My father came down with juvenile "type 1" diabetes at age 12, and it has been a major part of his daily life. My brother has struggled with intense, life-long pain and suffering since he broke his back in his twenties. We hear the pain of those who don't have enough work to do in order to make ends meet. I know people who are fighting cancer as I speak right now, such as my close friend in India who has leukemia. We see immigrants come through Los Angeles, hoping for a better life—trying to escape the long arm of the law so they don't get deported.

Furthermore, hundreds of thousands of desperate people sit at our southern border, trying to have the opportunity to live in the United States, a land of great promise. Almost everyone must go through their own version of trials and difficult times. It is apparent in all forms.

It is clear that life is hard. Here's what Peter says about it in verse 24:

> *"All people are like grass,*
> *and all their glory is like the flowers of the field;*
> *the grass withers and the flowers fall,*
> *25 but the word of the Lord endures forever."*

We're like grass. We will all grow old, fade, and eventually die. Our flesh will break down and go back into the dust of the earth. We will "wither," which is actually a pretty accurate description of the aging process. So, where's the good news in all of that?

The good news is this: as Christians, we have hope. And our hope is in the Word of the Lord. The Word of God has been preached to us (see 1 Peter 1:23). And we became "born again."

Pay attention to First Peter 1:22-23:

> *22 Now that you have purified yourselves by obeying the truth so that you have sincere love*

for each other, love one another deeply, from the heart. 23 For you have been born again, not of perishable seed, but of imperishable, through the living and enduring word of God.

So, how did the apostle Peter encourage the early Christians, who were under assault from the society around them? He told them to do three things:

1. Be holy ... be pure ... obey the teachings of the Word of the Lord.

2. Love one another ... from the heart. Love deeply. Be a loving person.

3. Know that your soul has an "imperishable seed" in it.

Maybe your body will wilt and turn to dust ... But your soul won't. C.S. Lewis famously said, "You don't HAVE a soul. You ARE a soul. You HAVE a body."

Your soul will enter the heavenly city, and you will shout with joy when you see your loved ones, when you see Jesus, and when you realize that you stood the test. You fought the good fight. You finished the race. You kept the faith. (2 Timothy 4:7)

Through it all, you remained faithful. And as Peter says, one day you will stand proud. And you will be filled with "inexpressible and glorious joy." And you will receive the end result of your faith: the salvation of your soul.

4. Speak Honorably
(1 Peter 2)

In this chapter, we are going to focus on something that each of us has to deal with: our speech. How we can use our mouths for God, and how we can stop using it for the devil. How did you do this week with your words? Did you praise and encourage somebody? Did you bless your children with affirmation? Did you sow joy and peace into the ears of your co-workers?

Or, perhaps times haven't been the easiest for you. Maybe you over-corrected your children, exasperating them. Perhaps you shouted a curse word at someone. Maybe you were harsh with someone in your orbit. Or maybe you reacted in anger at a person—damaging them in ways that are hard to repair.

If you did any of these negative things, then take heart. We have all been prone to use our tongues in ugly ways. We are human beings, and thus we are far from perfect, especially when it comes to our mouths. We shout at our children in unhealthy ways, we exaggerate the truth in order to drive home a point. Perhaps we take the Lord's name in vain sometimes. We speak poorly of people when they are not around. We brag on ourselves. Sometimes we give excuses when we ourselves know that we are not innocent. We slander people behind closed doors in order to "get some things off of our chests."

As much as we may do these things, the Bible says that they should not be done. These are sins. And we all need to be working on them.

In this chapter, we are focusing on 1 Peter chapter 2. This chapter begins with a pointed series of teachings aimed at helping us to clean up our mouths. Let's read 1 Peter 2:1-3:

> *Therefore, rid yourselves of all malice and all deceit, hypocrisy, envy, and slander of every kind. 2 Like newborn babies, crave pure spiritual milk, so that by it you may grow up in your salvation, 3 now that you have tasted that the Lord is good.*

This text begins with the word, "therefore." Anytime you see that word "therefore" in the epistles, you should perk your ears up, because something important is about to be stated.

What Peter is saying here, is that based on what he has just said (in chapter 1), he now has some fundamental teachings that we need to hear. He uses the word "therefore" because he has just been talking about holiness in chapter 1. He is urging us to "be holy in all that we do" (1 Peter 1:15). In chapter 1 he also urges us to "be holy, because God is holy" (1 Peter 1:16). What Peter is saying is that since our heavenly Father is holy, and we need to imitate God to the best of our abilities. We need to imitate Jesus as best as we can. Then he says, "Therefore."

And when Peter says "Therefore," he is saying, "You need to conduct yourself with holiness." Therefore... stop talking bad about people. Stop using "malice" against others. Don't think "malicious" thoughts, don't use malicious words, and do not act in malicious ways towards others.

Peter is also telling us to avoid being deceptive. If someone asks you something, be straightforward with them. Be completely truthful. Don't mislead. Your intentions should be pure.

Then Peter tells us to avoid hypocrisy. Don't claim to be a Christian, and then live a life that is at variance with the teachings of Christ. Be consistent in your life. Make sure your words and actions match your claims to Jesus Christ as your Lord.

Peter then tells us to guard against the very human propensity to envy others. It is natural to want things that others have, but repeatedly the Bible teaches us to avoid this way of thinking. In the 10 Commandments, it says, "Don't covet." That's the same thing. Don't wish you had the car, the house, the job, the spouse, or the body that another person has. This is normal human emotion, but God commands us to be different. Be content with what you have, and do the best with the things, and with the people, that God has blessed you with.

Then Peter tells us to "avoid slander of every kind." Now, this one tends to be a real challenge for people. Sometimes we slander people in indirect ways. We hear something about a person, and we repeat it, when we don't really know whether it is true or not.

Recently, I was with a group of guys in my neighborhood. We were sitting around enjoying each other's company. We were actually celebrating a guy's birthday, so a bunch of us dudes gathered to hang out. At one point in the conversation, somebody said something about a person. And one of my neighbors said, "Naw, I'm not gonna say anything about him. He's not here to defend himself." My friend actually said that twice that evening. And I thought to myself, "That's a great way to handle gossip!" Just say to yourself or to the person with you, "Let's not go there, he's not here to defend himself."

Let's face it, we are slanderous people sometimes. The definition of slander is to "make false and damaging statements about someone." Sometimes we try to hurt someone's reputation. This is so common, and it is so wrong. Let us avoid this kind of behavior. Let us eradicate slander from our lips.

At work, some people will speak ill of others, possibly because they want a promotion. So, the fastest way to get a promotion is to try to knock your competitors down a notch. Sometimes we get jealous of a person... try to defame them so that others will devalue them. This is all terribly wrong, and as Christians, we need to keep a *very tight rein* on our tongues when it comes to speaking ill of others. It is sinful to speak ill of other people, period.

As we move through 1 Peter chapter 2, we then encounter Peter making a contrast between those who follow Christ, and those who have chosen to disobey, or, stumble.

Peter speaks first about the disobedient, saying:

They stumble because they disobey the message—which is also what they were destined for.

9 But you are a chosen people, a royal priesthood, a holy nation, God's special possession, that you may declare the praises of him who called you out of darkness into his wonderful light. 10 Once you were not a people, but now you are the people of God; once you had not received mercy, but now you have received mercy.

Peter is telling us that those who "stumble" are those who live in the dark. They stumble around because they are disobedient. They hurt themselves by stumbling. They hurt other people because they stumble around aimlessly.

If we walk in the light, however, we don't stumble. Rather, we have purpose. We know exactly where we want to go. We don't hurt ourselves. There's a huge difference between walking around in the dark and walking in the light. When we live a life of slander and envy and malice, we have chosen to walk in darkness, behaving like non-Christians. When we walk in the light, we avoid such sinful ways of living and speaking.

You remember last chapter when we talked about living as "foreigners?" Peter returns to that theme again in 1 Peter 2:11-12:

> *11 Dear friends, I urge you, as foreigners and exiles, to abstain from sinful desires, which wage war against your soul. 12 Live such good lives among the pagans that, though they accuse you of doing wrong, they may see your good deeds and glorify God on the day he visits us.*

Peter is telling us here that we need to resist the ways of this world. This world is truly sinful. Just turn on the television, and you'll see a host of sins within only a few minutes, whether it is on Netflix or the evening news. When you look at your phone for the daily news, you are likely going to read *negative* news ... and very little positive news.

This world is "sin-sick." People are drunk on anger, they love dissension, and many people are full of lust and competitiveness and gluttony. It is truly a place where the Christian has to live as a "foreigner" or as an "exile." We don't belong here forever. Our eternal home is elsewhere, in Heaven. And we need to be careful that we don't start doing the things the world does. We need to be careful that we keep it clear in our heads that we, as Christians, are to resist the urge to follow the ways of the world. We must stay on the road that Jesus calls, "the straight and narrow."

The apostle Peter does something really important here in this text, chapter 2, verse 12. He is hinting at evangelism through living a holy life. He tells us to live such an upright life that people will be ashamed to accuse you of wrongdoing. You should live such a good, kind, righteous life that if someone accuses you of something, then the people around them will say, "No, not her. You're wrong on that one. She's not like that." People will go to bat for you. People will get your back if you live a righteous life. Even pagans will say, "Oh, yeah, he's actually a good person. I can't really speak out against him."

Peter is telling us that this is actually a way to evangelize. Live a righteous life so that the pagans and the sinners will open themselves up to the truth of the gospel simply because they know you are a righteous person who lives from conviction. People will notice a difference in you and wonder how to achieve that for themselves.

Peter then says something that is extremely relevant for us today. He tells us to honor the authorities, so that other people won't speak ill of us. He tells us to respect the people in governance so that the foolish slanderers will be silenced. Accusers won't have anything to say against us if we watch our mouths and only use them to build others up.

Here's what Peter says in 1 Peter 2:13-17:

> *13 Submit yourselves for the Lord's sake to every human authority: whether to the emperor, as the supreme authority, 14 or to governors, who are sent by him to punish those who do wrong and to commend those who do right. 15 For it is God's will that by doing good you should silence the ignorant talk of foolish people. 16 Live as free people, but do not use*

> *your freedom as a cover-up for evil; live as God's slaves. 17 Show proper respect to everyone, love the family of believers, fear God, honor the emperor.*

What Peter is saying here is that whoever the Emperor is—we should avoid speaking ill of him or her. We should realize that God is our true master. Our job on earth is to be respectful to *everyone*, and we should completely avoid speaking negatively about the people around us, including the political leaders.

Of course, the head political figure in Peter's time was the emperor. And on two occasions in that passage, Peter tells his readers to honor the emperor. And we can easily apply this teaching to us as well. We should *submit* ourselves to the authorities that have been established: the police, the courts, and the lawmakers.

We need to remember that we are not owned by those people; our deepest loyalty is to God. But God tells us to honor the secular authorities, whomever they may be. It is our responsibility to follow what God says, and thus, respect the authorities set in place.

I can guarantee you that there were emperors whose conduct was *far worse* than our own worst presidents. There were emperors who had people murdered, who were blatantly immoral, and who stopped at nothing in their lust for power. And let us remember that many of the emperors supported the persecution and even public execution of Christians.

In 1 Peter chapter 2, Peter talks about suffering for doing good. He tells us that we will likely suffer in this life. And then he says we have a clear path for how to handle this kind of situation. Why? Because Jesus was in the exact same spot. Jesus suffered for doing good. Peter says the following:

Christ suffered for you, leaving you an example, that you should follow in his steps.

22 "He committed no sin,
** **and no deceit was found in his mouth."*

23 When they hurled their insults at him, he did not retaliate; when he suffered, he made no threats. Instead, he entrusted himself to him who judges justly.

We may suffer in this life ... but imagine living in a world where Christianity is illegal. Imagine living in a world where nearly half of the population were slaves. Imagine living in a context where you have no rights. Christians in the Roman Empire rarely had Roman citizenship. They were often slaves. They were being watched by their masters. They were routinely abused, mistreated and disrespected.

And Peter is giving them the advice to follow Jesus's example. If you are disrespected, do not retaliate. Just as Jesus refused to retaliate, we should avoid retaliating. We should "make no threats" (v. 23). We should simply "entrust ourselves to God—who judges people justly."

As mentioned, the title of this chapter is "Speak honorably." I want to challenge you to make a transformation in your speech. Don't participate in conversations that bring others down. Don't participate in group slander. Don't lose your oral discipline. Don't allow your voice to be used to wreck the lives of others.

If they try to wreck *you*…then don't retaliate. Just realize that, as a Christian, you are not permitted to speak like that. Entrust yourself to God. Say to yourself, "Not my will, but thine." God judges justly. He will take vengeance on wrongdoers. *You will be vindicated.* You just have to trust…and obey your Heavenly Father. Speak honorably when you open your mouth. It is a hard lesson to master, but with the help of the Holy Spirit, we can do it.

5. The Functional Marriage (1 Peter 3)

Today's chapter is titled "The Functional Marriage." We are going to be looking at what 1 Peter 3 says about marriage, and how it is supposed to work, according to the Bible.

I think we all know that marriage can be difficult. It requires selflessness. It requires perseverance. It requires a steady willingness to offer grace and forgiveness. It requires a daily habit of looking for the best in your partner, rather than looking for areas that you can criticize. If you voice *all* of your criticisms of the person you live with, then you will have problems.

There is no fool-proof recipe for marriage. It is a lifelong obedience to God. You must be willing to set your own desires aside, and submit to the will of God, if you are going to make marriage work.

None of us were given a perfect example of how marriage works. We were all raised in less-than-perfect homes. Some of us were raised in outright dysfunctional homes. I would venture to say that very few of us were raised within an exemplary, once-married, stable, Christ-following household. In fact, statistics tell us that about half of marriages fail. Many of us were raised with one parent. Perhaps you had a stepparent. You may have had two or three stepparents over the years.

A couple of years ago, Sunde attended her father's memorial, and it was an opportunity for her to interact with several step-siblings she didn't know well.

Like Sunde, some of you were raised without a dad. Maybe you were abandoned by one of your parents when you were young. Some of you may have gone years at a time without speaking to one of your parents. Some of us were raised—or at least partially raised—by grandparents.

Some of you were born to married parents. And they stayed married throughout your life. However, even in those cases, there is a high probability that there was a fair amount of dysfunction. I am certain that most homes have issues that they are not proud of. We don't like to admit problems in our marriages, but it is necessary if we are going to address the areas where we can improve.

Both Sunde and I can tell you that marriage can be difficult at times. When she and I said, "I do," we meant it. For better or for worse. During those early years, we had no idea how difficult life can get sometimes. Marriages that last 28 years will get tested at some point.

No one gets a perfect marriage. No one. Even if you are blessed with a wonderful and loving marriage, there is a good chance you will have major challenges over the years. Maybe you have a child who dies young. Or you struggle with infertility. Maybe an affair occurs. A son or a daughter completely rebels against you. Your spouse suffers a major injury or illness. Perhaps one of you goes through a long period of depression.

There are so many things that can go sideways in a marriage. So many unforeseen things can happen. You grow apart. You have different takes on religion. Perhaps you go through periods where there's just not enough money—which happens to be one of the most common reasons for divorce. Maybe you had kids really young, and you just didn't have enough time, energy, or money to make it all work.

Things like the ones listed above prove that we don't have any perfect marriages because we don't have any perfect people. We are all flawed.

Let's not get too cynical, however. There is good news around marriage in American society. Marriage can be so fulfilling. It can be a place where you spur each other on to grow in faith, in your emotional life, and in your life satisfaction. Marriage provides a stable home for kids—where they can experience the joy of family. Marriage and family can be a *highlight of your life*, as it is for me!

And here's some *really* good news … if your marriage makes it to year 10, then you only have a 4% chance of getting divorced. That's right, just 4% of couples divorce after 10 years of marriage.[1]

---

[1] See Christy Bieber, "Leading Causes of Divorce: 43% Report Lack of Family Support," 15 August 2023, located here: https://www.forbes.com/advisor/legal/divorce/common-causes-divorce/.

So, the main point of this chapter is: how can we make marriages work according to the Bible? First of all, you have to live as a Christian. You must embody those things—in your own *individual* life—that God calls you to do. Remain humble and kind to your partner. Try to be selfless. Be generous with your time and money. Forgive often, and have grace daily on your partner.

These are things that Christians simply must do. You cannot live the Christian life if you refuse to forgive someone, or refuse to have grace on someone when they are imperfect. Having forgiveness and offering grace are fundamental parts of being a Christian.

In the text for this chapter, the apostle Peter is going to give us some good, sound advice on how to make *marriage* work. You know, some people today think the Bible's teaching on marriage is obsolete. They think that we must do what culture says about marriage. This is not true! God has written the Bible for people to follow throughout all of the time. The same things that the early Christians were told to do, are what we should follow.

We all know that the Bible has some pretty clear things to say about marriage. And let me emphasize this important point: *we reject God's Word at our own peril*. Sometimes even churches teach things contrary to what the Bible plainly teaches. They will say that the Bible was useful 2000 years ago, but we must enter the 21st century. They say that we need to listen to our culture more than we listen to the apostles or to the Lord himself. I admit … it takes real humility to obey the Bible.

Live Holy and Godly Lives: The Books of 1 and 2 Peter

It requires a lot of trust because sometimes the Bible's perspective is so *dramatically different* from the culture we currently inhabit.

Anytime the Bible contradicts our current culture, then I suggest we reject the culture and follow the Bible. Yes, American culture has some really good things in it, but our unique society will eventually fade away, like all cultures do. However, the word of God will still be around 10,000 years from now, should the Lord wait that long before He returns for His bride.

That's how all cultures work. They change and morph over time, and they often get assimilated into other, newer cultures. They don't necessarily disappear, since their values and customs may live on in various ways. For example, the Roman Empire fell in the year AD 476, but much of its culture is still with us.

I think we can all agree on this: the Word of God will last forever. And, as Christians, we should choose the Word of God over our present culture, or any culture for that matter.

So, what does God's Word say about marriage? Well, it says a lot. And we're going to focus on just that one section of scripture in 1 Peter 3:1-7, which deals explicitly with marriage. Let's look at the first six verses of that scripture, 1 Peter 3:1-6:

> *Wives, in the same way submit yourselves to your own husbands so that, if any of them do not believe the word, they may be won over without words by the behavior of their wives, 2 when they see the purity and reverence of your*

lives. 3 Your beauty should not come from outward adornment, such as elaborate hairstyles and the wearing of gold jewelry or fine clothes. 4 Rather, it should be that of your inner self, the unfading beauty of a gentle and quiet spirit, which is of great worth in God's sight. 5 For this is the way the holy women of the past who put their hope in God used to adorn themselves. They submitted themselves to their own husbands, 6 like Sarah, who obeyed Abraham and called him her lord. You are her daughters if you do what is right and do not give way to fear.

There are several lessons here, if you do a very careful reading of this passage. Let's break down the teachings and just list them out here:

1. Wives should submit to their own husband.

2. Christian wives can actually convert their non-Christian husbands to Christianity by their good behavior.

3. Christian wives should conduct themselves with purity.

4. Christian wives may be beautiful on the outside, but, by far, the *most important* thing is to be beautiful on the *inside*.

5. What does it mean to be beautiful on the inside? It means to have a gentle and quiet spirit. That is

"unfading" beauty, rather than external beauty, which is subject to fading over time.

6. Holy women of the past trusted in God. Holy women of today should do the same, just as their godly ancestors did.

7. Holy women of today should submit to their own husbands, just as the holy women of the Bible did.

8. Sarah trusted her husband Abraham, even when he made mistakes. But she stood by him and trusted him. Wives of today should do the same.

9. Wives should focus on doing what is right, and not give way to *fear*. Don't allow fear of others, fear of culture, or fear of the future cause you to turn away from your role—of being a faithful, righteous, and gentle wife.

Whoa! This does not sound politically correct, does it? This passage of scripture would surely offend people today. But, there again, should we conform to this world? Or should we try to trust in God's word? It is hard sometimes to trust in God's word, especially when society tries to push you in completely opposite ways!

Now, let's get to the second part of what Peter has to say on marriage. It is located in 1 Peter 3:7,

Husbands, in the same way be considerate as you live with your wives, and treat them with respect as the weaker partner and as heirs with you of the gracious gift of life, so that nothing will hinder your prayers.

So, what is this passage saying? Let's break it down:

1. Like in the previous section about wives, husbands, too, should be considerate of their wife.

2. Husbands should "live with" their wife. Unless you're in the military—or some such profession—my advice would be to try to follow what Peter says, and, to the best of your ability, live under one roof with your wife. There are distractions and temptations that will come your way otherwise. "*It is not good for man to be alone*," according to Genesis 2:18.

3. Husbands must "*respect*" the wife. She is weaker than you physically. But she is your partner. You are a team. You strengthen each other.

4. Husbands should *respect* their wife—God gave women "the glorious gift of life" just as God gave men life. So respect your wife as someone who received the gift of life from God. Don't be selfish. Realize that God put her on this earth just as much as he put you on this earth.

5. Finally, be considerate and respectful of your wife, "so that nothing will hinder your prayers." In other words, if you disrespect your wife, then the effectiveness of your prayers will be hindered. Of course, none of us want to pray weak or "hindered" prayers to God. Rather, we want God to hear our prayers and answer them. In order to have

effective prayers, we must respect our wives, and be considerate of them in all things.

We've just studied Peter's condensed advice on how to have a loving, *functional*, ideal marriage.

Peter devotes so much to the role of women in marriage and in the family because women play a central role in the family. And when you have a woman who trusts in the Word of God—rather than in culture—then you are a very blessed man. And your family will be strong.

It is so important that we, as Christians, understand the biblical model of the marriage covenant. Now, let's address the situation of a person marrying a non-Christian. Indeed, if a person marries a non-Christian, then it is *possible* the Christian will win the non-Christian to Christ.

However, the apostle Paul says in 2 Corinthians 6:14a, 15b, "Do not be yoked together with unbelievers... What does a believer have in common with an unbeliever?"

It is so important that we teach our children to marry Christians so that we have common ground in the covenant of marriage. So that we share the same values and core beliefs about supremely important matters such as morality and parenting.

Let's look back at the New Testament era for a moment—2000 years ago. Remember, in those days, Christianity was just getting started, and many women converted to Christianity first. We are told that women flooded into Christianity far faster than men did. Thus, it was quite common for women converts to Christ to be married to pagan, non-Christian men. And so, Peter has encouraging news. He says that the women can probably win that man over to Christ, if they live the life a faithfully committed disciple of Jesus. Living a life for Jesus sets a great example and will make others want to do the same.

On the man's side, husbands were the head of the household in Greco-Roman times. They were the *paterfamilias*. They were the person who made transactions, and who kept the family secure on a material level. They were not only physically stronger, but they were much stronger than women socially.

And Peter is cautioning men that they need to respect their wives, and be considerate of their needs and desires. This would have been a strange concept for a pagan to think about, as pagans viewed their wives differently than that. Church history tells us that so many women joined the church precisely because of what they saw happening in Christianity: women were respected, widows were taken care of, orphans were adopted, and infanticide was prohibited. Women who married Christian men tended to be in a *much* better situation than the wives of pagan men. Christian men were highly sought after, due to their reputation for being honorable and respectful with their families. Even though they were still the "paterfamilias" (the Roman concept of the husband being the head of the house), they were gentle and *good* with their wife and children.

Getting married is easy. It entails a short ceremony, and a signed piece of paper. But *living the institution of marriage*—the Christian way—is difficult. It requires discipline, thoughtfulness, and mutual respect.

Again, I urge you … don't listen to culture on this topic. We must focus on obeying the word of God, and what it says about marriage.

6. The Eyes, Ears, and Face of God (1 Peter 3)

"The eyes of the Lord are on the righteous and his ears are attentive to their prayer." This verse is found in Psalm 34:15, and quoted again in 1 Peter 3:12.

This chapter will continue our dive into the Petrine Epistles, or 1 and 2 Peter. Our scripture reading is from 1 Peter 3:8-17.

> *8 Finally, all of you, be like-minded, be sympathetic, love one another, be compassionate and humble. 9 Do not repay evil with evil or insult with insult. On the contrary, repay evil with blessing, because to this you were called so that you may inherit a blessing. 10 For,*
>
> *"Whoever would love life, and see good days, must keep their tongue from evil and their lips from deceitful speech.*
> *11 They must turn from evil and do good; they must seek peace and pursue it.*
> *12 For the eyes of the Lord are on the righteous and his ears are attentive to their prayer, but the face of the Lord is against those who do evil."*

13 Who is going to harm you if you are eager to do good? 14 But even if you should suffer for what is right, you are blessed. "Do not fear their threats; do not be frightened." 15 But in your hearts revere Christ as Lord. Always be prepared to give an answer to everyone who asks you to give the reason for the hope that you have. But do this with gentleness and respect, 16 keeping a clear conscience, so that those who speak maliciously against your good behavior in Christ may be ashamed of their slander. 17 For it is better, if it is God's will, to suffer for doing good than for doing evil.

This is an extremely practical section of scripture that is very encouraging. We could focus on many of the teachings here. Just for starters, here are a few of the ideas Peter is trying to get across to us in this reading:

- Have compassion on the people in your life.

- Be humble towards people, and get along with others. Don't fight with others, or seek to "get them back" when they offend you.

- Don't sin with your mouth. We all have to work on this one. Whether it is gossip or cursing or the occasional outburst at people. Peter is clear: we should not use our speech for sinful purposes.

- Do good. God's eyes are on you if you live righteously. But God will oppose you if you do evil things.

I know the natural response for some of us is to fight. We often assert ourselves and express our opinions. Some of us struggle with forgiving people. We are the type that wants to "get them back." We stew at night, thinking about how we can get revenge on the person who humiliated us, or cheated us, or borrowed and didn't repay. We make plans in our heads about what we're going to tell them. We might even take steps to plot something against them.

Let's say it like it is today—there is a basic instinct within some of us—those who are natural-born fighters. We are justice oriented. We feel like if you do something wrong against us, then there is a price to be paid. For whatever reason—our childhood, we got picked on in school, or we are just sick and tired of being bullied—whatever it is, some of us learned on the playground this famous passage from *3 Corinthians 19:6*: "Do one to others before they do one to you."

Does this describe some of you? Are you the type that likes to get back at people? Have you ever plotted against another person? Perhaps you took steps against that person who slandered you, or questioned you, or disrespected you, or tried to make you look like a fool?

Well, if this describes you, then let me point you to the words of Peter, once again:

> *13 Who is going to harm you if you are eager to do good? 14 But even if you should suffer for what is right, you are blessed. "Do not fear their threats; do not be frightened." 15 But in your hearts revere Christ as Lord. Always be*

prepared to give an answer to everyone who asks you to give the reason for the hope that you have. But do this with gentleness and respect, 16 keeping a clear conscience, so that those who speak maliciously against your good behavior in Christ may be ashamed of their slander. 17 For it is better, if it is God's will, to suffer for doing good than for doing evil.

Some of you have very little gentleness when you get into arguments with people. Some of us tend to disrespect others on occasion, especially when they've disrespected us in front of others. And so, we have to reclaim our self-respect (at least in our own eyes).

But this is precisely what fools do.

Recently, I pulled out my Bible and read from Proverbs. And one thing that popped out at me time and time again is that God punishes fools. God punishes those who choose to do the wrong thing, and those who go against the teachings he has put into place in His word. For instance, Proverbs teaches, repeatedly, these three things:

1. that God sets His face against the person who thinks evil thoughts.

2. God works against the person who plots evil against another person.

3. God detests the prideful person.

Proverbs 15:25a reads, "The Lord tears down the proud man's house."

Hebrews 10:31 puts it another way, "It is a dreadful thing to fall into the hands of the living God."

So what is Peter getting at in our scripture for this chapter? I think Peter is giving us a rationale for why we need to be faithful disciples of Jesus. Peter is looking out for us. He is teaching us to be very careful how we think about others. Often, thinking bad thoughts about someone is the beginning step in taking action against someone. This is why Jesus says the crime of murder begins with the sin of anger. Adultery begins with lust. And so on.

Peter is protecting us. He is saying that we need to be careful what we ponder. Be careful of those hateful thoughts. Be careful of targeting someone in your mind, and thinking ill of them. God opposes that kind of person. God will not be as open to your prayers.

And one thing you need to pick up on in this passage is the logic that Peter uses. Peter says that *we should suffer* for doing good because *Jesus* suffered for doing good.

Jesus was so countercultural. When people hit him, he blessed them. When people cursed Jesus, he forgave them. When they mocked him, he prayed that God would forgive them due to their ignorance of what they were doing.

In other words, Jesus does not ask you to do something that He is unwilling to do. Kings may do that. Presidents may do that. They will send you into battle, but will earthly political leaders send *their own son* into battle? Not likely.

You see, this is what separates the King of Kings from the kings of men. Human leaders are often hypocrites. They'll tell you to do something that they don't intend to do themselves. This is the sign of a bad leader: they say one thing yet do another. It's called hypocrisy.

But God is different. God sent *his own son* into the world. That's a far cry from worldly leaders. Rather, God shows us how to live by first doing it himself. This is what is *so revolutionary* about Christianity.

The book of 1 Peter was written at a time of persecution. The Christians were being laughed at by others. Their leader was publicly crucified. Christians were considered weirdos because they followed a crucified Lord. It must have been terrifying for our brothers and sisters who were put to death for holding on to their faith.

In many ways, we are living at an amazing time for Christianity. Yes, I realize that the world is often very dark, and sometimes it seems we are surrounded by forces hostile to New Testament Christianity. But in many ways, we are living in a wonderful time. Nobody opposes us for attending church services or reading our Bibles. We don't have people ratting us out, or turning our names in, or removing our civil rights on account of being Christians.

However, let's not be naïve. Even here in America, many of the tenets of our faith don't sit well with the culture. There are times we will believe things that the entire culture seems to disagree with us on. There are times when the path of Jesus and His apostles will get us into trouble. I'm not surprised at all whenever I hear of Christians being maligned in the news or on social media because of their disagreement with the general social and moral trends in Californian—or American—culture.

Our culture can be very fickle. One decade they think this, and the next decade they think something totally different. This is why we root ourselves in the solid Word of God. Our beliefs don't fluctuate like that. God is a rock, a solid and stable presence in our lives. He does not shift and morph like culture does.

However, at times—I can pretty much guarantee—you will find your beliefs don't match the beliefs of the culture around you. And you will face consequences of some sort. And these can be very difficult moments for us as Christians. Now, let's not exaggerate. We are not going to be burned in the flames for believing the teachings of Paul or Peter. But … we just might lose out on a job because of our beliefs. We just might burn some bridges because of our faith in Jesus.

The point that I want to hit hard in this chapter is precisely what Peter hit hard in his sermon, in 1 Peter 3:14-15:

> *14 But even if you should suffer for what is right, you are blessed. "Do not fear their threats; do not be frightened." 15 But in your hearts revere Christ as Lord.*

Do not fear other people. Do not be frightened by people's words, threats, or actions. Don't fear others. Rather, fear God.

Why? Because God has his eyes on you. Peter says this:

> *12 For the eyes of the Lord are on the righteous*
> *and his ears are attentive to their prayer,*
> *but the face of the Lord is against those who do*
> *evil.*

I want each of you to tuck away something in your heart: God knows you. God's eyes are on you. He is aware of those good deeds you have done. He hears your cries for help, cries for mercy, cries for intervention.

- God saw you when you gave some extra money to that person ... and *nobody else* will ever know.

- God saw you when you chose to pray for the person who was trying to pick a fight with you.

- God noticed when you chose to walk away—when you could have returned insult for insult.

- God noticed when you sat down with your Bible and read from Proverbs, or from 1 Peter, or from James or Paul or Genesis.

- God was pleased with you when you knelt down in prayer when you were alone in the house.

- God surely noticed when you became a "fisher of men"—when you invited your friend or neighbor to church.

- God noticed when you stopped yourself before you said those curse words. You could have said them. But you held your tongue.

What is my point? My point here is that God notices your good acts. God loves the fact that you are trying to be a disciplined person. You are noticed by the Creator of the universe. Your good deeds are not ignored. They are not done in total secrecy because God sees you. Your good deeds are plain as day to the Lord. He sees you, and He will reward you. Call on the name of the Lord. Live righteously for Him—and you will see good things happening in your life.

But if you choose to go against God ... if you choose to rebel against God's authority ... if you become arrogant and think you are better than the next guy ... God's face will be against you. And it's not because God hates you. No, God doesn't hate us when we make mistakes. Rather, the reason we experience consequences for our sins is because of something we read about in Hebrews 12:6: "God disciplines those whom He loves." Just as a good parent disciplines her children, so our heavenly Father disciplines us whenever we rebel.

Like I said at the outset of this chapter: Peter is giving us some extremely practical teaching here. I remember when I was first coming to Christ. I was in college. I was raised in church, but I did not become a *Christ follower* until my college years. And, friends, my favorite book right whenever I began my journey—it was 1 Peter.

1 Peter chapter 3, in particular, spells out some of the most basic lessons of living the Christian life. There are many teachings there. I know some of you like it whenever I provide a short list of "take homes." I don't want to overwhelm you with 26 take homes today—as there are so many teachings here. But I will offer a short list of two of my favorites from today's text. I'm going to pluck them out and offer them to you:

1. God blesses your obedience. He gives you surprise gifts in your life.

2. God's face is against those who do evil.

Let's all realize these truths that are attested throughout the Holy Scriptures, and especially here in 1 Peter.

Something that we all know is that living as a disciple of Jesus is not easy. But I can promise you one thing—you will never regret it. There is nothing quite like the feeling of living for Jesus, walking in His light, and enjoying the abundant blessings that God will send your way.

7. This Water Symbolizes Baptism (1 Peter 3:18 – 4:11)

Do any of you remember your baptism? For many of you, it was probably many years ago. You may have had a conversation with your parents after hearing a lesson at Sunday School. Or perhaps you came to Christ later in life, after thinking hard about the meaning of life, and how you could be redeemed from your sins. Or maybe you got baptized alongside some of your friends at a summer church camp.

I faintly remember my own baptism. I was 11 years old. And I was the grandson of the preacher who established the church where I grew up, the Southside Church of Christ in Portales, New Mexico. My grandfather was well-known in that town, as he served as a minister there for around 60 years. Baptism at a young age was kind of expected of me. I was raised in the church. I had attended Bible Class all throughout the years in our Children's ministry. In addition to his preaching duties, my grandfather also served as one of the elders. There was a time when my dad served as a deacon, and he also led singing frequently at the church.

Many of the people around me insinuated that I might be the next preacher in the family. I loved my grandfather and followed him around a lot. He was truly a role model to me. Early in my life, I gained a deep appreciation for church ministry, and for the wonderful role a minister could play in a faith community.

So, one day, during the "invitation song," I decided to make my way up to the front pew. And I would declare my faith in Jesus Christ, which I did. My grandfather took my "great confession" and he baptized me that day. It was a glorious day for me. I still believe that my heart was in the right place—well, for an 11-year-old.

Looking back, however, I believe I probably should have waited a little longer, until I could truly make an informed decision that I wanted to follow Christ rather than the ways of the world. When you're 11 years old, and raised in a Christian family, you just haven't been exposed to a whole lot. You think you want to serve God with your life, and do the right thing, but you haven't really been tested by the fires of temptation, or by the schemes of the Devil.

The decision to follow Jesus is, by far, the most important decision a person will ever make in life. If you choose to follow Jesus, your life changes. Your destiny changes. Your future is shaped in dramatically different ways than if you choose not to follow Christ. You will choose to marry a devoted Christian. You will put your faith and family first—way above everything else. You will become a certain kind of person—one who lives for Jesus. You will take a job that will not conflict with your core convictions. Your friends will be, mostly, Christians. You will get close to your church family because they will be your inner circle—the people you can trust. Your church friends will probably be the ones you open up to whenever life throws you curveballs. Church friends become your "brothers" and "sisters." Your faith will shape every aspect of who you are. You will hear God's Word every Sunday. You will worship Him in the assembly every Sunday. You will look at the first day of the week as "the Lord's Day." *You'll pray daily*.

This chapter, we are going to focus on 1 Peter chapters 3 and 4. The precise text is 1 Peter 3:8-4:11. We are going to deal with a part of scripture that discusses the importance of baptism. It has become fashionable in the Christian world to downplay baptism. Some people like to say that salvation doesn't really require baptism. Their logic is that it is God's grace that saves us. Nothing can get us to heaven. We are saved by grace, not by works. They *overemphasize grace* to the point that the believer isn't really expected to do much. In this view, baptism is simply an outer sign of something that goes on inside the heart.

Now, it is true that God saves us because he has grace on us. We are all saved by grace through faith, just as the apostle Paul points out repeatedly. We are saved by God's grace and not by works, so that we cannot boast in our own righteousness. These are teachings are, indeed, from the apostles.

However, where people go astray is when they downplay baptism. I truly get concerned when people say that baptism is not necessary. They think baptism is an optional ritual that has little bearing on the state of your soul. According to scripture, however, baptism seems to be is essential in the life of a disciple of Jesus. In the New Testament, baptism was simply assumed.

Baptism is critically important in the life of a believer. Pay attention to these:

- Jesus *himself* submitted to baptism; he was baptized by John the Baptist.

- Jesus *preached* about baptism. In John 3:5, Jesus stated, "Very truly I tell you, no one can enter the kingdom of God unless they are born of water and Spirit."

- Jesus commanded his apostles to baptize believers. After Jesus resurrected, he said these words, his last words on this earth, in Matthew 28:19: "Therefore go and make disciples of all nations, baptizing them in the name of the Father and of the Son and of the Holy Spirit."

- We also know that the apostles were baptized. For example, when Paul turned to Christ, in Acts 9:18, we are told, "At once, something like scales fell from Saul's eyes, and he regained his sight. Then he got up and was baptized."

- We also know that the apostles preached that followers of Jesus should be baptized. Peter himself said these words in Acts 2:38, "Repent and be baptized, every one of you, in the name of Jesus Christ, for the forgiveness of your sins. And you will receive the gift of the Holy Spirit."

I've often wondered: *Why would anyone downplay baptism when Jesus and the apostles all became baptized, they all preached about baptism, and they all baptized those who came to faith in Christ?* Why would anyone omit or even downplay this important part of the Christian faith? It should be a *big celebration* in the life of people who unite themselves to Jesus!

Well, I think today's lesson in 1 Peter helps us to understand the *context* of baptism.

Now, first ... it is true that some people get baptized without being conscious or authentic believers. There are people who get baptized mainly because they want to marry someone who demands that they get baptized before the wedding. Yes, these kinds of things happen. There are people who get baptized as babies, or as young children, and completely stray from the faith as adults.

But let us not throw out the baby with the bathwater (*did you get that!*). Baptism is essential. It is immensely significant in the Bible. It is something that is understood—if you come to Christ, then you get baptized.

Here is what Peter says in 1 Peter 3:18-22:

> *18 For Christ also suffered once for sins, the righteous for the unrighteous, to bring you to God. He was put to death in the body but made alive in the Spirit. 19 After being made alive, he went and made proclamation to the imprisoned spirits— 20 to those who were disobedient long ago when God waited patiently in the days of Noah while the ark was*

being built. In it only a few people, eight in all, were saved through water, 21 and this water symbolizes baptism that now saves you also—not the removal of dirt from the body but the pledge of a clear conscience toward God. It saves you by the resurrection of Jesus Christ, 22 who has gone into heaven and is at God's right hand—with angels, authorities and powers in submission to him.

In this section of 1 Peter chapter 3, Peter is trying to teach his readers that baptism is part of the *process that saves you*. As he says, "This water symbolizes baptism that now saves you also." I've heard people say, "Baptism doesn't save you." Well, Peter says here, verbatim, that baptism does save you. However, he's not talking about simply dunking yourself in a lake, or merely taking a bath. That's why Peter says, "Not the removal of dirt from the body."

Rather, true baptism is when someone makes a "pledge of a clear conscience toward God." And baptism has the power of salvation in it because, as Peter explicitly says in verse 21, "baptism saves you by the resurrection of Jesus Christ."

So here's my question … Why would someone downplay baptism if it is so closely associated with salvation in the New Testament? To be honest, I don't really know.

Jesus and the apostles clearly emphasize that we should emphasize the sacred power of baptism. When it is done right…when it is done with a "clear conscience toward God"…when it is done in the name of Jesus Christ…and when it is done consciously by the one making the personal commitment.

Indeed, when a person is baptized, just as Jesus says in John 3, they are "born again."

Let's move on to our next passage of scripture here in 1 Peter. Please look with me at 1 Peter 4:1-6:

> *Therefore, since Christ suffered in his body, arm yourselves also with the same attitude, because whoever suffers in the body is done with sin. 2 As a result, they do not live the rest of their earthly lives for evil human desires, but rather for the will of God. 3 For you have spent enough time in the past doing what pagans choose to do—living in debauchery, lust, drunkenness, orgies, carousing and detestable idolatry. 4 They are surprised that you do not join them in their reckless, wild living, and they heap abuse on you. 5 But they will have to give account to him who is ready to judge the living and the dead. 6 For this is the reason the gospel was preached even to those who are now dead, so that they might be judged according to human standards in regard to the body, but live according to God in regard to the spirit.*

Peter is teaching us here that when a person comes to Christ, they must be committed to living a righteous life. Yes, we are saved by God's grace. But whoever argues that righteousness is unnecessary is preaching a foreign gospel. The teaching of the apostles is that we who proclaim Christ must live pure and holy lives. We must be aware that we will be judged by the Lord. Therefore, we live differently than the pagans do. They often live wild lives, and sometimes they even disrespect us for living a life of righteousness, devoted to our faith.

Indeed, Christians are today frequently scorned in the media. Sin has become so rampant, that Christians are often seen as prudish or strangely "judgmental" when they choose to live according to the dictates of the Christian faith.

But don't let this bother you. And certainly don't let it deter you. Persecution will come. You will be judged for being a Christian. It is not a matter of if, but when. You will face scrutiny for holding close to Christ when the world beckons you to follow its sinful and wayward paths.

And these are things the new Christian needs to be aware of. Think twice before descending into the waters of baptism. You are making a major commitment.

Finally, Peter says some things to encourage us, in 1 Peter 4:7-11:

> *The end of all things is near. Therefore be alert and of sober mind so that you may*
> *pray. 8 Above all, love each other deeply, because love covers over a multitude of*
> *sins. 9 Offer hospitality to one another without grumbling. 10 Each of you should use whatever gift you have received to serve others, as faith-*

ful stewards of God's grace in its various forms. 11 If anyone speaks, they should do so as one who speaks the very words of God. If anyone serves, they should do so with the strength God provides, so that in all things God may be praised through Jesus Christ. To him be the glory and the power for ever and ever. Amen.

People will always speculate about when the end of the world will be. Ultimately, only God knows, but the Bible teaches that we are living in the last days. "The end of all things is near." There are two ways to think about this. First, Jesus teaches that He will return at a time that will basically catch everyone off guard. It will be "like a thief in the night." We won't be expecting His return.

But there is another way to think about this context of "the end is coming soon." We may die in a car accident, or from a brain aneurism, or a rapidly progressing illness. We will all die, and it will be sooner than we probably imagine. Given the grand sweep of history, a few decades is nothing to the Lord. The end is coming soon. Like James teaches, we are like vapor—here today, gone tomorrow.

Therefore, Peter argues, we must remain *sober*. We should pray often. Give meaningful love to the people in our lives. Offer hospitality to people who need it. We must not grumble with each other. Rather, we should serve the people around us, willingly using our gifts to help people. We should speak words that benefit people

… encouraging and godly words. In all things, we should praise the Lord and give the glory to Jesus Christ. Speak openly about the Lord, and how He has saved you. Just as Bobby did—on the first day of class—whenever I met him. I will never forget that. It is hard to speak so openly about your passion for Jesus Christ whenever you are surrounded by cool and trendy college students.

I think we all know these things that Peter is preaching to us today. I think we all understand that we need to be baptized. I think we all know that baptism is by both "water and Spirit" and one without the other is nonsense. Baptism without the heart is nothing more than taking a swim. Baptism without the water is playing with fire. Why refuse to follow the prescription for baptism that Jesus and the apostles taught and lived?

Peter teaches us today that Christianity is not all that complicated. Love strongly! Be hospitable! Remain sober. Speak honorably to other people. Praise God often!

These are all lessons that we know deep down within us. But, certainly, it is a struggle sometimes. We all have our battles with anxiety, with depression, with sin, with arrogance, and with emotional and physical pain. Following Christ does not require great brilliance, but it does require great humility, and discipline. Following Jesus means to "take up thy cross." We are told to follow Jesus' example and live as he lived. It won't be easy, but it will be worth it!

8. How to Suffer Well
(1 Peter 4:12-19)

I heard about a Jewish lawyer who was very troubled by the way his son had turned out. And, like any good Jew, he went to talk with his rabbi about it.

The lawyer said to the rabbi: "Dear rabbi, I brought my son up in the faith, I gave him a very expensive bar mitzvah. It cost me a fortune to educate him at Hebrew University. Then, last week, my son tells me that he has decided to become a Christian! Rabbi, where did I go wrong?"

The rabbi said, "Funny you should come to me! Like you, I also brought my son up in the Jewish faith. I put him through Yeshiva to study the Torah. It cost me a fortune! Then one day, *my son, too*, comes and tells me he has decided to become a Christian."

The lawyer asked the rabbi, "So, what did you do?"

The rabbi responded, "I did what any good rabbi should do. I went to God and asked him for his opinion!"

With great expectation and wide eyes, the lawyer asked the rabbi, "Please tell me, rabbi, what did God say to you?"

The rabbi replied, "It was really strange. When I asked God what to do about my son becoming a Christian, He said, 'Funny you should come to me…something very similar happened with my son!'"

Now this may sound like a silly story, but it's important that we recognize the meaning behind it. When you come to Jesus … when you make Jesus the Lord of your life, you are going to feel a joy that you've never experienced before. You will experience the Creator of the universe, living inside of you through His Holy Spirit.

However, your Christian life will also come with challenges, just as the Bible teaches. And the books of 1 and 2 Peter are largely about this situation. They were both written around the time of Nero's reign, when a bloody cycle of persecution was launched against the Christians. And many were asking, "Why are we suffering? How are we supposed to handle such horrible opposition?" The early Christians suffered just for being Christians!

Today's scripture gives us advice on how to suffer well. Our scripture, from 1 Peter 4:12-19, tells us how we can deal with our own challenges better. We don't have to live life being defeated by our challenges. We can face our difficulties with optimism, with hope, and even with joy. As a Christian, our outlook should be good, even when things around us are painful or disorienting.

God's word is going to give you answers to the problems you are facing. You just need to pay attention carefully to *how God says to suffer well*.

Live Holy and Godly Lives: The Books of 1 and 2 Peter

First of all, in 1 Peter 4:12, we read this verse:

12 Dear friends, do not be surprised at the fiery ordeal that has come on you to test you, as though something strange were happening to you.

Let's stop right there for a second. I think often we feel like we are going through something strange when we suffer. Sometimes we feel like life isn't fair.

- Someone hasn't returned our call in several days, and we feel flat out ignored. It really hurts if you thought you were good friends!

- Or, your health has been bad for a long time.

- Or, you feel burdened by the worries of this life … you're getting weary … and it is starting to get to you.

- Or, you have people in your life with whom you've had a disagreement, and you don't really know how to deal with the situation.

In response to these situations, the apostle Peter says to you, "Welcome to being human! You're not going through something strange. It's normal."

Peter is absolutely correct. Whatever you find yourself going through, know this: *it is common*. You are *suffering*. You are *struggling*. Perhaps all is not well in your family or with your health. "Welcome to the club," Peter says!

What is Peter's solution? Here it is in 1 Peter 4:13-16,

13 But rejoice inasmuch as you participate in the sufferings of Christ so that you may be overjoyed when his glory is revealed. 14 If you are insulted because of the name of Christ, you are blessed, for the Spirit of glory and of God rests on you. 15 If you suffer, it should not be as a murderer or thief or any other kind of criminal, or even as a meddler. 16 However, if you suffer as a Christian, do not be ashamed, but praise God that you bear that name.

Did you catch it? Peter gives us the following advice in this passage. Here's what you should do when you are going through challenges and trials:

- "Rejoice"
- "Be overjoyed"
- "You are blessed"
- "God rests on you"
- "Do not be ashamed"
- "Praise God"

As you probably realize, Jesus gave very similar advice during His earthly ministry. He said, in Matthew 5:3-12 – in what is often called "the Beatitudes":

3 Blessed are the poor in spirit, for theirs is the kingdom of heaven.

4 Blessed are those who mourn, for they will be comforted.

5 Blessed are the meek, for they will inherit the earth.

6 Blessed are those who hunger and thirst for righteousness,

for they will be filled.

7 Blessed are the merciful, for they will be shown mercy.

8 Blessed are the pure in heart, for they will see God.

9 Blessed are the peacemakers, for they will be called children of God.

10 Blessed are those who are persecuted because of righteousness,

for theirs is the kingdom of heaven.

11 Blessed are you when people insult you, persecute you and falsely say all kinds of evil against you because of me. 12 Rejoice and be glad, because great is your reward in heaven, for in the same way they persecuted the prophets who were before you.

Why would God want us to rejoice and be glad? Why would God want us to be *joyful* when we are suffering?

Here's the answer: *God's people have always struggled.* You're not going through anything strange. This is normal. *Don't panic.* You are dealing with normal challenges.

The reason this is helpful is because *God never promised to remove suffering from your life.* Suffering is necessary. Suffering is all around us; it is part of the world we live in. And those of us who are Christians need to let our light shine *despite the grey clouds and the challenging times* we must deal with.

But remember this: *God wants you to rejoice.* Praise Him in the midst of this storm. It is your choice. You can mope around and get angry at people. You can hang your head and be depressed if you want to. But that's not what God wants you to do. God wants you to be *positive*. He wants you to be *resilient*. He wants you to realize that *you are actually blessed* because you are in a relationship with Him. Nothing will conquer you. Nothing will overcome you. Nothing will defeat you.

As the apostle Paul said, "For to me, to live is Christ, and to die is gain" (Philippians 1:21). In other words, not even death can destroy you. Paul realized that when we get to Heaven, all of our suffering will cease. So, *even death* is something to be embraced.

So how is Peter's advice to us today helpful? It is helpful because it is quite obviously *the better way* to respond to challenges. If you allow a grey cloud to follow you around, who are you going to help? How can you serve God if you lay in bed, defeated, for days on end?

Get up! Get out there and smile. Be thankful that God will walk you through this storm. Like a great athlete, you should welcome the challenge. Stand up and face it. Be courageous! Don't cower down and allow the depression to defeat you! *Don't go into a downward spiral.*

Life is all about *perspective*. *You choose* how you are going to respond to your situations in life. Some people choose to be *sad*, even when they have a good home, plenty of money, plenty of good food, and people who love them.

But you, don't be like that! Don't follow that miserable path. Surround yourself with people who will speak *positivity and joy* into your life. If you do happen to end up in the presence of a person who is all negative and toxic, then try to *turn them around*. Tell them they need to think differently. And if they won't, then you probably need to create some space between you and them. Life is hard enough; don't allow others to bring you down with them.

I want to conclude with 1 Peter 4:17-19. This is how Peter ends the chapter. He says,

> *17 For it is time for judgment to begin with God's household; and if it begins with us, what will the outcome be for those who do not obey the gospel of God? 18 And,*

"If it is hard for the righteous to be saved, what will become of the ungodly and the sinner?"

19 So then, those who suffer according to God's will should commit themselves to their faithful Creator and continue to do good.

Peter is saying that your responsibility is to continue doing good, because you are part of the Lord's household.

The key to "suffering well"—which is the title of today's sermon—is to "continue to do good." Be faithful to your Creator. Suffer "according to God's will."

Think of the history of God's people. They often suffered when they followed God. And we will likely have to do the same.

Have you ever watched a movie, and the good guy punches the bad guys, and we all feel good because that vengeance satisfies something deep down in us? Well, that's not the way the Lord asks us to deal with our challenges. You can't beat up everyone who wrongs you. You can't punch everyone who insults you. It is totally ungodly to destroy the people who insult you or disrespect you. As a Christian, you need to "suffer well." Suffer like Jesus suffered. He *prayed* for them. He *forgave* them.

Jesus refused to see himself as a *victim*. Rather, he was a *victor*!

He was resilient. And the key to resilience is to realize that everybody goes through this stuff. You're not the only one with broken relationships. You're not the only depressed or anxious person in the room. Peter says in verse 12, "Don't think something strange is happening to you."

Instead, adopt a more positive mindset. Realize that you have two choices: you can get down and depressed, or you can choose to push through it. Don't be a victim. You're suffering just like everybody else suffers.

Be strong and courageous. Life is hard. If you let it, life can knock you out. People can be so cruel. But Peter urges you to rise above.

But don't just put on a smile, you need to "continue to do good" as Peter says in verse 19. Find something good to do for someone!

Get out of bed, face your struggles, defeat them in the name of Jesus. Things will eventually turn around, as they always do.

Don't get bogged down in the negative. It is a dead-end street. Don't get hopeless. It won't help you at all.

Think about what Peter advises in today's scripture: be joyful that God created you. Be "overjoyed." When people insult you, realize that God will bless you. Choose to live a joyous and courageous life. Get out there and do something good for somebody ... and let God take care of the rest.

9. Respect for Elders
(1 Peter 5:1-6)

In this chapter, we are going to delve into the fifth and final chapter of the Epistle of First Peter. We will talk about the importance of *respecting our elders*.

I begin by talking about India. Some of the most formative memories in my life have occurred in India. I travel there fairly regularly, as much of my academic work has dealt with religion in India.

And one of the most important observations I have made during my years interacting with India is this: Indians respect their elders deeply. They respect authority. They value the people in their society who are older. It is very common for Indians to live in multigenerational families, all inside one home. Some of us in America may shriek at that thought! Living with your in-laws … ALL THE TIME! Sounds more like Purgatory, doesn't it!

However, it is customary in Indian society for the newly married woman to move into the home with her new husband's family. She becomes part of his family. This is one reason that many people say India is a patriarchal society. Not only does the woman's family have to pay a dowry, but the woman's family also loses out on the deal because their daughter effectively becomes one with her husband's family.

I have mixed emotions about how they do it in India. On the one hand, it is really sad to me that someone with girls has to become almost punished for having girls. This is why there is a famous blessing in India from woman to woman that goes like this: "May you be the mother of a thousand sons."

On the other hand, it is helpful for a newly-married couple to have the support of an older, wiser couple. Ideally, the system works. When new babies come along, the grandparents play a critical role, as they are always there to help out. It is extremely common in India for people to be very, very tight with their grandparents, as their grandparents literally helped raise them. I can relate to this a bit, since I was super close with my own grandparents, yet on my mother's side.

In the church context, Indians are very respectful of the Shepherds who are tasked with looking after the flock. They respect the older men, as well as the older women, who have served the Lord for many years. Indian society in general has an uncommonly high regard for teachers. This all goes back to the caste system, where the teachers—known as the Brahmin caste—were the highest echelon of the society. Thus, teachers have always been highly respected—even revered—in Indian society.

Pastors are deeply trusted in India. They are relied upon whenever there is a new baby, a funeral, or a house-cleansing (yes, the minister always comes in and prays in a new home in order to purify it and dedicate it). Pastors are always brought in when it comes to marriage, as the Indian system has arranged marriage. They are often an important resource for helping to connect families together for the marriage. I was surprised to learn that pastors often name children.

All of this points to the deep respect that Indians have toward authority. And in the Indian mind, authority comes from two sources: one's role in society, and one's age.

It is amazing for me whenever I teach at seminaries in India. When a teacher so much as enters a room, the students all stop talking, and they typically stand up. They will only sit down whenever the professor signals that they should sit down. This does NOT go on in the United States—as if I had to remind you!

Similarly, Indian students are reluctant to speak out in class, in case they might speak out of order, causing any sort of problem for the professor. This is significantly different from the American context, where students are often very eager to express their views. Indian students are rather shy in the classroom, even when called upon. In the American scene, students often express their views with great conviction. Indian students, however, don't really have a culture of doing that. So when an American instructor, like myself, calls on a student, Indian students will stand up, and then clam up. I try to put them at ease, but I also need to be respectful of the Indian approach to education. As Indians see it, the teacher is supposed to do the talking, whereas the students are there to learn, not really to express themselves.

One class I taught in India held a party for me at the end of the semester, and presented me with a trophy, with an engraved expression of thanks. I was floored. And they truly meant it. They all gave me kind and sincere words, thanking me for spending the semester with them. It was so heartwarming and encouraging for me to experience that! If any of you have ever taught or preached or anything of that nature, it is so encouraging when someone takes just a minute to say "thank you."

Indians are also deferential towards people older than them. I have seen very few exceptions to this. Indians just naturally respect people who are older than them—even slightly older. This is not unique to India, as I have witnessed the same phenomenon in other parts of Asia as well, especially Korea and China.

In East Asia, scholars attribute this deep respect for elders to the teachings of Confucius. In my world religions lectures, I teach about Confucius. He lived about 500 years before Jesus, and one of the cornerstones of his teaching was that you must respect your elders. This plays out in a variety of ways.

For instance, in Asia, it is not very common to have senior homes. People move in with their families whenever they lose their spouse, or if they become physically unable to be independent.

I have heard that American-style elder homes are just now starting to pop up in China, but in India, this is extremely uncommon. People move into the home of their children. That is considered the natural course of things.

At Pepperdine University, where I teach, one of my neighbors is a Sikh family, from India, and they have moved their parents—from India—into their own home there on the Pepperdine campus, as is expected in Indian society.

The Bible is very strong on this point. *You shall honor your elders.* The 10 Commandments make it clear that you should *honor your father and your mother.* Rebelling openly against one's parents is a deep and painful sin in the Bible. God organized humans in such a way that we need to respect our elders, and we really get ourselves out of order when we violate this principle.

This chapter's Bible passage is 1 Peter chapter 5. Let's read verses 1-6:

> *To the elders among you, I appeal as a fellow elder and a witness of Christ's sufferings who also will share in the glory to be revealed:*
>
> *2 Be shepherds of God's flock that is under your care, watching over them—not because you must, but because you are willing, as God wants you to be; not pursuing dishonest gain, but eager to serve;*
>
> *3 not lording it over those entrusted to you, but being examples to the flock.*
>
> *4 And when the Chief Shepherd appears, you will receive the crown of glory that will never fade away.*

> *5 In the same way, you who are younger, submit yourselves to your elders. All of you, clothe yourselves with humility toward one another, because,*
>
> *"God opposes the proud*
> *but shows favor to the humble."*
>
> *6 Humble yourselves, therefore, under God's mighty hand, that he may lift you up in due time.*

We must point out that elders, too, bear responsibility to make this social contract work. Elders are to be "shepherds" in the church, for example. Shepherds must take special care of the people that are under their charge.

There should be a spirit of *willingness* in elders. They should be people of deep integrity, eager to serve others. Like Jesus. He was the Lord, but he was also a servant among servants. It is amazing that Jesus actually bent down and washed his disciples' feet—illustrated so passionately in the 2023 (Chiefs vs. 49ers) "He gets us" Christian Super Bowl ad.

Similarly, elders in the church should not "lord it over" the flock, but be kind, gentle, and respectful of them. Everyone should have respect and humility toward one another. There should be an overall "spirit" of respect & humility.

For those who are younger, Peter has direct words: "You who are younger, submit yourselves to your elders." When the younger folk start rebelling against the older folk, it rocks the boat in unhealthy ways, and eventually, it could overturn the whole thing.

We've seen this happen before: for example, in Communist China, in the Great Leap Forward, which lasted from 1958 to 1961. The youth were commanded by Chairman Mao Tse Tung to openly rebel against—and mock—the older generations. The older people were dragged out into the streets, and forced to wear dehumanizing signs and "dunce-like" hats. Many of them were shipped off to work camps. The youth were given a *carte blanche* to rule the nation.

When I think about the American context, I am not trying to be judgmental. It is simply my sense that we in America do not respect our elders like they do in India, or Africa, or even Latin America. American society seems to privilege youth over age. We even have a word for this now days, called "ageism," which is what happens when people discriminate against the elderly in various ways. Perhaps an elderly person is not as savvy at computers, so they get marginalized in the workplace. As Christians, we need to be very careful that we are inclusive of elderly people, and realize that all age groups have their place in the kingdom of God. Young and old, the church is made up of many parts, and all must be respected.

We have a great need for elders—or, "shepherds"—and other forms of authority in the church setting.

We always need to be working towards the biblical model of leadership in the church. And what did the early church have? They had evangelists, elders, deacons, and teachers, as well as others.

What does this mean when I say we need to always be working towards the biblical model of leadership? This means that we always need to keep our eyes open for men who can serve our congregation as elders. We also need to be on the hunt for deacons—those who will serve selflessly, taking pressure off of the elders so that they can focus their attention on shepherding souls. We must always rely on God's spirit as we seek His will for our church family.

Let's come back to where we began. Let us all show deep humility in our lives, especially towards our elders. Let us shower them with grace and hospitality. Let us honor our fathers and our mothers. Let us revere our grandmothers and our grandfathers. Let us show proper respect towards the people in our lives who are older than us. Because once we start clawing down the order that God has established, then our cultural fabric will begin to break down.

That being said, however, those who are older must conduct themselves with respect and great humility, too. Being an older person means you should be more seasoned in the faith. You should help to pass on the legacy of serving Jesus Christ as Lord.

All of us who have crossed into—or who are crossing over into—the "elder" phase of our life should serve others with honesty and servanthood, just as Peter says in v. 2. Perhaps most importantly, the elders should "be an example to the flock."

Let us all be people who show respect to our elders. And elders, let us be people who are worthy of the respect of our younger church members.

And finally, let us all conduct ourselves in such a way that we draw others to Jesus—the *Chief Shepherd*. By bringing others to Him, we will be showing our utmost respect to Jesus Christ—the lover of all souls. We are but His servants, entrusted with the task of reuniting people with their Creator.

10. Confirm Your Calling (2 Peter 1:1-11)

In this chapter, we are going to start diving into 2 Peter. Remember, both Petrine Epistles were written by the apostle Peter, who was one of the core members of Jesus's ministry team of 12 men. Peter is deeply revered among the world's Christians. This has been the case for nearly two millennia. The Roman Catholic Church, in particular, holds Peter in extremely high regard, and they recognize him as their first Pope. As Protestants, we don't hold to the notion of a papacy, but like the Catholics, we also hold Peter in high regard. Peter was clearly one of Jesus's closest friends on this earth, and we should take his teachings very seriously. He was a proven disciple of Christ, and he was also a martyr who died for his faith in Jesus.

This chapter is entitled "Confirm Your Calling." What do we mean by "Confirm Your Calling?" What we mean is this: you were called by God. Did you know that? God called you. You were at one time lost, but now you are found. You had no direction. You were going through life aimlessly.

At one point, some of us were even prone to fall into many sins, such as rage, unforgiveness, substance abuse, sexual license, and arrogance. Some of us may even have used physical violence on people. Some of us strayed from the Lord and did things that we now regret. We may have used bad language, told lies, and perhaps we spoke maliciously of others behind their back. As the Bible puts it, we were lost. We were like a ship without a rudder. Now, that's the bad news.

But here's the good news. Each one of us here today turned our backs on those sins. At least we are trying to turn our backs on those behaviors because we were called by God, out of darkness, and into the light of Jesus Christ. We turned away from our lies, our sins of the flesh, our sins of the mind, and our sins of omission. We *repented*—the very word repent means to turn around. We turned around and started walking in the light, just as Jesus is in the light. God called us. He called us to be His disciples. He called us to be His ambassadors in this often-depraved world. God called us to a *different standard*—that is the standard of the New Testament. At this stage of our lives, many of us are trying to live like the New Testament would have us live. We are doing our best to "confirm our calling."

The title for this chapter comes from 2 Peter 1:10, which says,

> *10 Therefore, my brothers and sisters, make every effort to confirm your calling and election.*

The Bible teaches that we are saved by God's grace (Ephesians 2:8). That is true. He has grace on us and forgives us. However, the key to unlocking God's grace is our faith in Him. And we all know that faith without works is dead (James 2:17). James makes this very clear when he says, "You see, then, that a man is justified by works, and not by faith only" (James 2:24).

Similarly, in Peter's words, we must "make every effort" to confirm our calling. We live our lives doing good works so that we confirm our Christian identity.

In 2 Peter 1:5-9, the apostle says we should …

> *Make every effort to add to your faith goodness; and to goodness, knowledge; 6 and to knowledge, self-control; and to self-control, perseverance; and to perseverance, godliness; 7 and to godliness, mutual affection; and to mutual affection, love. 8 For if you possess these qualities in increasing measure, they will keep you from being ineffective and unproductive in your knowledge of our Lord Jesus Christ. 9 But whoever does not have them is nearsighted and blind, forgetting that they have been cleansed from their past sins.*

This is an important passage here. Peter emphasizes that Christian faith takes effort. Salvation does not come easy. Just as Peter said in 1 Peter 4:18, "If it is hard for the righteous to be saved, what will become of the ungodly and the sinner?"

In other words, living the Christian life takes effort. It is not like we are "called" and then live on easy street.

No, we have to put in effort. It is often said that it takes 10,000 hours before you achieve mastery in something.

- Do you think musicians magically learn how to play beautiful compositions?
- Do you think Steph Curry came out of the womb with a 92% free throw shooting percentage?
- Did Stephen King become a great writer without tossing away thousands of pages of improvable texts?

Of course not. These people worked hard. They got out of bed each day, made a schedule, practiced constantly—while most people scrolled on their phones—and they got busy "running down a dream" (to borrow a phrase from Tom Petty). It took untold hours of work for them to get where they eventually got.

It is very similar with us as Christians. You are not going to be a great disciple of Jesus if you don't put some effort into it. You are not going to "achieve" if you don't cultivate some discipline in your life.

This is true with so many things in life. You want to be a great husband or wife to your partner? It takes work. Want to be a great mom or dad? It takes hours of investment into your child's life. Thousands of hours, actually.

Peter challenges us in 2 Peter 1:8 that we should avoid becoming "ineffective and unproductive in our knowledge of our Lord Jesus Christ." Rather, he challenges us to live with "increasing measure" lives of self-control, perseverance, godliness, and love. He tells us in 2 Peter 1:9 that we must not forget that we have been cleansed from our past sins. Those painful memories of our walking in sin should motivate us to live our lives enthusiastically for Jesus.

We all want to flourish. Want our lives to be full of success and happiness. And the way we flourish is by living our faith, just as Peter outlines in today's text. He uses such choice words: faith, goodness, godliness, perseverance, mutual affection, and love.

When we flourish, we don't just satisfy our own needs, we imagine the future of the Lord's work. We will pass away, just as the Bible teaches. What legacy are we leaving behind? The book of James (4:14) says: What is your life? For you are a mist that appears for a little time and then vanishes.

Jesus calls us to be "fishers of men," fishers of people. When we fish for people, not only are we answering the Lord's call that we seek and save the lost, but we are also bringing new life into our church communities.

I think COVID-19 gave us all some time to reflect. I hope we haven't completely forgotten how nice it was to come back, and hug one another again. That era was a brutal one for me, personally. I am a people-person. And I was so sad during that time. For many of us, our mental health deteriorated, as our social lives virtually stopped. We longed to see each other face to face. We longed to see one another with love in our eyes, and with warmth in our hearts.

But I hope that ghastly COVID-19 era also gave us a chance to count our blessings. To remember how joyful it is to gather together, to share meals together, to commune together, and to flourish together as a community.

And now is our chance to "reboot." Let's figure out ways to be "effective and productive" in our faith. Let's evangelize our neighbors, baptize new Christians, and get excited about living the Christian life again after that frozen era that we recently came through. Let's rebuild and rejoice, knowing that God has us in his hands.

In 2 Peter chapter 1, the great apostle gives us a list of things we need to do in order to "Confirm our Calling." We should:

- Be truly good people. Practice goodness. Be good to people.

- We must gain knowledge. Those of us who teach in the local church can help in this department. Let's keep on preaching the Good News and educating people in the things of God, as long as we have breath in our lungs.

- We must practice self-control, Peter says. Have you ever lost self-control? Have you ever completely lost it? Have you ever shouted degrading things at somebody? Let us be on guard for this kind of terrible behavior! If we do these things, then we have surrendered ourselves to the Evil One during that moment, and we have ceased to practice self-control. This is a huge part of Christian discipleship.

- Perseverance is also on Peter's list here. Have you ever given up? You live the Christian life for a short time, and then throw up your hands? Sometimes we even decide to return to the sins that we thought we had left behind. Peter addresses this issue in 2 Peter 2:22, when he tells us not to return to our sins like a dog returns to its vomit.

- Peter then tells us we need to practice "godliness" (v. 7). This means just what it says: "What would Jesus do?" But here's one important thing about godliness: you have to know God. And the way you get to know God is through a relationship with Him. You pray to Him. And you read and study His word.

- Then Peter urges us to practice "mutual affection and love." These are consistently singled out as the most important aspects of being a Christian. If we cannot practice mutual affection and love, then we are not living the Christian life. And, yes, sometimes this is hard. Like when someone has hurt you badly. Like when someone has turned against you, or abandoned you.

- Friends, Christian love is the most important thing … yet it is one of the hardest things for many of us. It takes work … like shooting a lifetime of free throws, just as Steph Curry has. It takes deliberate practice if we are going to improve at it.

Friends, in today's passage, in 2 Peter 1:8, Peter tells us this:

If you possess these qualities in increasing measure, they will keep you from being ineffec-

tive and unproductive in your knowledge of our Lord Jesus Christ.

I think all of us want to be "effective and productive" in our Christian walk. We all want to be participants in God's great plans for what He wants to do in this world.

We all would like to be "effective and productive" Christians. Where we move and flourish, rather than stagnate. Too many churches are stagnating today. Instead of being comfortable in our lives, let's move to bring more people to Christ.

Once we start effecting and producing ... then we will see growth, vibrance, and flourishing. We will see more new cars pulling into our parking lot on Sundays. We will see the classrooms filling up with children. We will see God doing great things through us in this community. We will have new voices coming into our midst to praise God during our assemblies. We will have fellowship with new people, as we seek and save the lost. We will welcome people, many who have probably not been part of a faith community before. We will encounter people who are hurting, people who are in need, people who have so much to offer if they just found a community to serve in.

I want to close this chapter with a line that you may have missed, in 2 Peter 1:1. Peter refers to those who "... have received a faith as precious as ours."

We have a precious faith. It is precious. Let's use this faith, that we have been blessed with, to "confirm out calling". We are called to do great things for God. Let's not hesitate because we don't think we have what it takes. God tells us that, through him, we have everything we could need. You've been called. It's time to confirm that calling.

11. Remember These Things (2 Peter 1:12-21)

This chapter is going to focus on the passage 2 Peter 1:12-21. If you haven't already gathered, Peter was a special person in the estimation of Jesus. He was a key part of Jesus's inner circle, and almost every important event in the gospels features Peter as a witness or participant. Peter's teachings are of inestimable work, and I give thanks to God that he lived long enough to write down some of his observations and teachings.

Also, you may not know that the Gospel of Mark is thought to be written by Mark, yet from Peter's perspective. This would make a lot of sense since Mark is believed to be the earliest Gospel. Peter's perspective was, and is, crucial for us having a better insight into the life, work, and teachings of Jesus. Peter's thoughts are crucial because they give us a front-row seat into the mind and motives of Jesus. We certainly get to hear from someone who knew Jesus well, walked with him, and sat at his feet through the ministry of our Lord. Only the apostles James and John could claim to know Jesus more personally than Peter. Of course, Jesus's mother, Mary, would be part of that inner circle, too. But Peter's perspective is critical.

This chapter is called, "Remember these things," and is from a text in our reading, 2 Peter 1:15: And I will make every effort to see that after my departure you will always be able to remember these things. Peter is telling us to remember the life of Jesus, remember the Lord's teachings, and remember what it was like to be in Jesus's presence.

It is really an awesome thought that we get this close perspective from Peter—a man who was right there to experience and see and hear all of the wondrous and miraculous scenes from the life of Jesus. And Peter urges us to "remember these things" because they are so important for us if we are going to follow Jesus. Peter wants us to review the scenes from Jesus's life. He wants us to recite them, to meditate on them, and to keep them at the forefront of our minds. I have no doubt that this would have been a true exercise for Peter himself. He experienced all of these things with Jesus as a fairly young man, probably in his late 20s and maybe early 30s. And by the time of writing 2 Peter—probably 30 or 35 years after Jesus died, that is, around the late 60s AD—Peter's memories would have been crucial for the church to have in its possession.

When you open up your Bible and read from 2 Peter, you have a great treasure in your hands. It is a true gift from God that we have 1 and 2 Peter. But I suppose that Peter would have been particularly urgent to ensure that the teachings of Jesus, and the scenes from Jesus's life, were properly remembered. That is why Peter was so adamant that we "remember these things."

Now, let's read the beginning of our passage: 2 Peter 1:12-15:

> *12 So I will always remind you of these things, even though you know them and are firmly established in the truth you now have. 13 I think it is right to refresh your memory as long as I live in the tent of this body, 14 because I know that I will soon put it aside, as our Lord Jesus Christ has made clear to me. 15 And I will make every effort to see that after my departure you will always be able to remember these things.*

In this passage, Peter is driving home the central point that we must not forget: We must remember. He tells us a few important things in this passage:

1. He will continue to remind people about Jesus until the day he dies.

2. He will continue to refresh people's memories about the life and times of Jesus, as Peter realized his time on earth was coming to an end.

3. Peter acknowledged that his hearers were "firmly established" in the truth, but he would continue to preach the gospel as long as he could.

4. Peter wants to make sure that the gospel—the teachings of Jesus and the teachings about Jesus—would last long after Peter's "departure" from this life.

There is no better motive for a Christian, than to keep preaching the gospel until death. To keep reminding the people around you of Jesus. To do everything you can to ensure that these teachings get passed on to the next generation. There is no nobler cause on earth than this one: keeping the gospel alive for future generations. That is why I have titled this chapter "Remember these things."

Why does Peter want us to remember these things? Why are we commanded to sit in church every Lord's Day, hearing teachings about Jesus Christ? Why do we pause every Lord's day to think about the importance of Jesus's death? Why do we pass down all of these old stories that have been told for thousands of years? You may wonder to yourself, "Why do Christians do this? Why does the preacher get up there and keep teaching about the life of Jesus *over and over and over again*? What's the point?"

The point is this ... These are the sacred teachings from God that will deliver salvation to your soul. That is what is so important about the teachings. That is the most urgent application of the biblical witness.

You and I want to live beyond death. We want everlasting life. And if we know the gospel, if we believe the gospel, and if we allow the gospel to transform our hearts, then we will be saved from hell, and from everlasting death.

But there is a secondary point here as well. The teachings of the Bible can help your life in the here and now, too. The life of Jesus can teach you to overcome the evil in your life with good—a lesson that is so obvious, but so difficult to live out.

The Eucharist, the Communion, is crucial to us as Christians, not just because the body and blood of Jesus give us eternal life, but because our current lives in the flesh are improved in the here and now when we take time to consider the cross. We have extraordinary unity, as fellow believers in Jesus Christ, when we gather around the table. There is an eternal dimension, but there is an earthly dimension, too. And you cannot separate the two dimensions from each other. As Jesus said in the Lord's Prayer, in Matthew 6:10, "On earth as it is in heaven."

What do we mean by this? What do we mean when we say, "You cannot separate the eternal dimension from the physical dimension?"

As Christians, what we mean is this ... our present lives impact our eternity. Jesus will reward us based on the things we have done in the flesh. He will reward us based on how we responded to his teachings when we lived upon the earth. We will not have a relationship with Jesus in eternity if we have no relationship with Him on earth. "On earth as it is in heaven." The two realms are integrally connected. There is no "one" without "the other." *You will be in Heaven, dear friends, because you came to know Jesus while on this earth.*

And Peter understands all of this. He wants us to rehearse the teachings of Jesus. He wants us to "remember these things." He wants us to gather on the Lord's Day—each and every single week—in order to "refresh our memories" as long as we are in the flesh. He wants us to teach these things to our children, to put them by our bedsides, to think upon the life of Christ with regularity so that *we might enjoy eternity with him.*

It is extremely important to understand the past. If we don't rehearse our history, then we are doomed to repeat the mistakes of the past. We learn from history. We learn what not to do. We learn what is important to preserve. And we learn the crucial story that God created man so that man could become eternal, like God. It is all interrelated, both heaven and earth coexist and intermingle.

The second paragraph (2 Peter 1:16-18) in our excerpt of 2 Peter goes like this:

> *16 For we did not follow cleverly devised stories when we told you about the coming of our Lord Jesus Christ in power, but we were eyewitnesses of his majesty. 17 He received honor and glory from God the Father when the voice came to him from the Majestic Glory, saying, "This is my Son, whom I love; with him I am well pleased." 18 We ourselves heard this voice that came from heaven when we were with him on the sacred mountain.*

What is Peter talking about here? He is talking about a scene in the gospels known as "the Transfiguration." This story is found three times in the gospels, for example, in Mark chapter 9. This story is about a time when Jesus took Peter, James, and John with him up on a high mountain, and he was transfigured before them.

His clothes became dazzling white. And at that moment on the mountain, Moses and Elijah—the great Old Testament prophets—appeared to them, and talked with Jesus. Peter was absolutely frightened on that occasion. And then a voice from Heaven said, "This is my Son, whom I love. Listen to him!" (Mark 9:7)

For many centuries, since the early church, this amazing scene has been called "the Transfiguration"—as Jesus was "transfigured" before Peter, James, and John—the three closest friends of Jesus.

Interestingly, Peter recollected that scene in this text here in 2 Peter. It proved to Peter that Jesus was the fulfillment of all Old Testament prophecy. It proved to Peter that Jesus was truly God's Son. If there was any doubt in Peter's mind about the power and authority of Jesus, then this took care of it. Peter was utterly amazed by the scene, and he ensured that it was recorded in the Gospel of Mark.

This is an example of Peter remembering, and passing down, the story to us. He wanted us to remember this scene. Peter points out that the teachings of Jesus are not myths. They are not fanciful. They are not made up. Peter screams in this text, "We were eyewitnesses of his majesty!"

(2 Peter 1:16)

This is something important that separates Christianity from other religions. Other religions tell us that gods fought with each other, or that the sun is a god, or that some gods are animals, or that you are one with the universe, and so on. But the difference in the *Christian* message is that it was historical. It is not some weird half-cat God that we worship.

We have the testimony of eyewitnesses. This is history. And this is what separates Christianity from the other religions.

The final passage from Peter today is 2 Peter 1:19-21:

> *19 We also have the prophetic message as something completely reliable, and you will do well to pay attention to it, as to a light shining in a dark place, until the day dawns and the morning star rises in your hearts. 20 Above all, you must understand that no prophecy of Scripture came about by the prophet's own interpretation of things. 21 For prophecy never had its origin in the human will, but prophets, though human, spoke from God as they were carried along by the Holy Spirit.*

Peter uses this paragraph to increase our confidence in the testimony of the apostles. He says the teachings *of* Jesus, and the teachings *about* Jesus, are "completely reliable." And "you will do well to pay attention to it." The Christian gospel will shine upon your life, as light can dispel the darkness. The teachings of Jesus will bring light to your heart, soul, and mind. You will think more clearly. You will be full of *good* news, rather than toxic, self-defeating ideas. You will speak words of hope and encouragement, rather than words of doom and gloom. The hope that is found in Jesus Christ will liberate you from the effects of sin.

In this paragraph, Peter is telling you and me that the teachings of the apostles and prophets are not human in origin. They are from the Holy Spirit of God. You can trust them! They are bedrock and foundational. You can *build your house* on these teachings.

Peter's teaching is wonderful in this text. As he says, "Remember These Things." Here are three things to remember:

1. "Refresh your memory." This line comes from 2 Peter 1:13. In other words, read your Bible. Go to church. Continually keep your memory "refreshed" by the teachings found in God's Word.

2. Peter was an eyewitness to Jesus. This is very strengthening for our faith. And that is precisely what Peter wants to do. He wants his testimony about Jesus, and about events like the Transfiguration, to build up our faith. Peter says, "I was there, folks!"

3. We have the gospel! Peter says, "We have the prophetic message!" That should be very exciting for you. That's why you have light in your eyes. That's why your life is not dark and depressing. You are "a light shining in a dark place," just as Peter says. Jesus says something very similar in the Sermon on the Mount. Here's what he says in Matthew 5:14-16: "You are the light of the world. A town built on a hill cannot be hidden. Neither do people light a lamp and put it under a bowl. Instead, they put it on its stand, and it gives light to

everyone in the house. In the same way, let your light shine before others, that they may see your good deeds and glorify your Father in heaven."

I want to close this chapter by encouraging you to revisit the teachings of the Bible often. Read them. Sing them. Recite them. Memorize them. Teach them to others. And have full confidence that not only will these teachings lead you to a better life, but these teachings will save your soul.

Again, let us "Remember ... These ... Things!"

12. Watch out for False Teachers
(2 Peter 2)

Our text for this chapter is 2 Peter chapter 2, the entire chapter. This text is not about blue skies and rainbows. This text is a repudiation of false teachers, and it gives us some tips on how to spot them.

The word of God is not all positive. As you well know, there are depictions of grievous sinfulness—and consequent punishment—such as at Sodom and Gomorrah. There are times when God lashes out at human beings such as with the Tower of Babel, the Flood, the destruction of the Israelites in the desert, and the "Passover" which featured the Angel of Death. And, of course, there is a coming scene of hellfire where people will be punished, where there will be "weeping and gnashing of teeth" (Luke 13:28).

It would be irresponsible for us to focus only on the rainbows, when the whole point of the flood story was massive destruction. In Genesis 6:5-8 we read of God's motives for the flood:

5 The Lord saw how great the wickedness of the human race had become on the earth, and that every inclination of the thoughts of the human heart was only evil all the time. 6 The Lord regretted that he had made human beings on the earth, and his heart was deeply troubled. 7 So the Lord said, "I will wipe from the face of the earth the human race I have created—and with them the animals, the birds and the creatures that move along the ground—for I regret that I have made them." 8 But Noah found favor in the eyes of the Lord.

Put another way, it would be irresponsible of me to write about heaven while neglecting the reality of hell. In fact, Jesus himself teaches us this, in Matthew 7:13-14:

13 Enter through the narrow gate. For wide is the gate and broad is the road that leads to destruction, and many enter through it. 14 But small is the gate and narrow the road that leads to life, and only a few find it.

Well, in 2 Peter we have one of those difficult chapters in the Bible that describes the reality of false teachers, and how you can identify them. Why is this important? Why does God's Word warn us about these kinds of teachers? I think there are three major reasons:

1. To prevent the church from falling under the power of Satan, thereby losing its ability to lead people to

Heaven. The church needs to remain pure and spotless, like a bride (the church) awaiting her groom (the Lord Jesus).

2. To remind us that there are in fact people out there who will use the preaching and teaching of God's word for sinful means. Their hearts are not right. Their motives are bad.

3. To keep preachers and regular churchgoers on their toes, keeping them mindful of what a sinful and crafty teacher actually looks like so that we will only choose honorable individuals to lead our churches.

The passage begins with a bang. In 2 Peter 2:1-3, we read the following:

> *But there were also false prophets among the people, just as there will be false teachers among you. They will secretly introduce destructive heresies, even denying the sovereign Lord who bought them—bringing swift destruction on themselves. 2 Many will follow their depraved conduct and will bring the way of truth into disrepute. 3 In their greed these teachers will exploit you with fabricated stories. Their condemnation has long been hanging over them, and their destruction has not been sleeping.*

This first passage tells us that *there will be false prophets and false teachers.* They will come. They are out there. Beware. They will introduce heretical teachings, such as denying the sovereignty of Jesus. They will say Jesus was "just a man." They will have "depraved conduct." Jesus also warned about these people when he said in Matthew 7:16, "By their fruits you will recognize them." These people will bring shame onto the church, with scandals and immorality. These teachers will "fabricate stories" and will "exploit you" by trying to get you to follow their foolishness.

But take heed. They will be destroyed. And so will we if we follow them.

The second paragraph here is 2 Peter 2:4-10a:

4 For if God did not spare angels when they sinned, but sent them to hell, putting them in chains of darkness to be held for judgment; 5 if he did not spare the ancient world when he brought the flood on its ungodly people, but protected Noah, a preacher of righteousness, and seven others; 6 if he condemned the cities of Sodom and Gomorrah by burning them to ashes, and made them an example of what is going to happen to the ungodly; 7 and if he rescued Lot, a righteous man, who was distressed by the depraved conduct of the lawless 8 (for that righteous man, living among them day after day, was tormented in his righteous soul by the lawless deeds he saw and heard)— 9 if this is so, then the Lord knows how to rescue the godly from trials and to hold the unrighteous for punishment on the day of

*judgment. 10 This is especially true of those
who follow the corrupt desire of the flesh and
despise authority.*

In this passage, Peter tells us about the realities of hell. Some of Satan's angels are currently being held there. This is one of the reasons for why there is a hell—there was a rebellion in heaven led by Satan, and it has led to a long battle between the forces of good and the forces of evil.

Peter reminds us that God does indeed have a vengeful side to Him. This is a well-known fact of both the Old and New Testaments. In Romans 12:19, the apostle Paul quotes Deuteronomy 32:35, when he says this:

*Do not take revenge, my dear friends, but leave
room for God's wrath, for it is written: "It is
mine to avenge; I will repay," says the Lord.*

2 Peter reminds us that just as God unleashed His wrath in ancient times, he will do so again. However, let us keep in mind that God always protects those who have a relationship with Him. God always saves those who trust in Him. God always provides a refuge for those who "Do justice, love kindness, and walk humbly in the sight of God" (Micah 6:8).

Peter then discusses Sodom and Gomorrah—two cities that became overridden by sexual sin. God burned them up, and saved only Lot—"a righteous man"—and his family. Lot was "distressed" by all of the wickedness he saw around him, and God provided him a way out of the fiery destruction. Peter tells us that, for a long time, Lot (Abraham's nephew) was deeply troubled by all of the sexual sin going on in those depraved cities, and it "tormented his righteous soul" for many years. Finally, however, God destroyed the wicked people of those cities, and saved Lot.

Have you ever been troubled by the profound amount of sexual sin—like Sodom and Gomorrah—going on around us? If so, then please stand firm. God will destroy those who indulge themselves.

But please, do not get seduced. Do not bow down to sexual license and promiscuity. Let us be warned by the Holy Scriptures: those who embrace the wickedness of this world, as with Sodom and Gomorrah—they will be destroyed. Our salvation is at stake. The future of our souls is at stake. Our eternal afterlife is at stake.

Peter tells us that God will "rescue" us, however, if we hold on to our righteousness, and not give in to the sinful world around us. Stay clean. Stay pure. Because destruction is coming upon those who rebel against God. Just as destruction is coming to Satan one day, it is also coming to those humans who "despise God's authority." Peter singles out here "those who follow the corrupt desire of the flesh." Let us live pure and righteous lives, as God commands us to.

The third paragraph in today's text, 2 Peter 2:10b-12, says:

> *Bold and arrogant, they are not afraid to heap abuse on celestial beings; 11 yet even angels, although they are stronger and more powerful, do not heap abuse on such beings when bring-*

*ing judgment on them from the Lord. 12 But
these people blaspheme in matters they do not
understand. They are like unreasoning animals,
creatures of instinct, born only to be caught
and destroyed, and like animals they too will
perish.*

Peter warns us that the people who rebel against Almighty God will perish. God will wipe them out. Like animals, they will get caught and destroyed. God will punish them severely, just like he punishes the "bold and arrogant." People who "blaspheme" will regret it one day when they stand before the throne of God to be judged. "Blasphemy" is when we are sacrilegious—when we defame God. Blasphemy is what people do when they show no respect to the Creator, nor to His son, Jesus Christ. Those who blaspheme are particularly prone to the wrath of God.

Here is the fourth paragraph in 2 Peter 2, verses 13-16:

*13 They will be paid back with harm for the
harm they have done. Their idea of pleasure is
to carouse in broad daylight. They are blots
and blemishes, reveling in their pleasures while
they feast with you. 14 With eyes full of adultery, they never stop sinning; they seduce the
unstable; they are experts in greed—an accursed brood! 15 They have left the straight
way and wandered off to follow the way of Balaam son of Bezer, who loved the wages of
wickedness. 16 But he was rebuked for his*

wrongdoing by a donkey—an animal without speech—who spoke with a human voice and restrained the prophet's madness.

Those who have harmed others will receive justice. They will receive the harm on themselves that they have inflicted on others.

Peter condemns those people who "carouse" around in the daytime. They feast and get drunk and commit adultery. Like a sin-infused party, they are only seeking pleasure. They are always on the lookout for an opportunity for fornication or adultery. "They never stop sinning." These people "seduce the unstable."

They look for people who are struggling emotionally. They look for people who lack confidence. They are on the hunt for people to take advantage of. Peter refers to these people as "an accursed brood." They are cursed snakes. They have completely abandoned the straight and narrow path to heaven and have given themselves to the wickedness that is as old as the Old Testament story of Balaam, who was rebuked by a donkey. The wages of wickedness—the wages of sin—they lead to destruction. And we have been warned, according to Peter.

The final paragraph—2 Peter 2:17-22—continues thus:

17 These people are springs without water and mists driven by a storm. Blackest darkness is reserved for them. 18 For they mouth empty, boastful words and, by appealing to the lustful desires of the flesh, they entice people who are just escaping from those who live in error. 19 They promise them freedom, while they themselves are slaves of depravity—for "people are slaves to whatever has mastered them." 20 If they have escaped the corruption of the world by knowing our Lord and Savior Jesus Christ and are again entangled in it and are overcome, they are worse off at the end than they were at the beginning. 21 It would have been better for them not to have known the way of righteousness, than to have known it and then to turn their backs on the sacred command that was passed on to them. 22 Of them the proverbs are true: "A dog returns to its vomit," and, "A sow that is washed returns to her wallowing in the mud."

Peter condemns these sinful people. They are accursed to the "blackest darkness" of everlasting hell. They will be consigned to eternal death.

These people boast, but their words are empty. They are full of lust for the flesh of other people—always looking for someone to feast their eyes on. They entice people who are trying to escape the sinful snares of this world. We've all known "new Christians." These false teachers will prey on new Christians because the new Christians are still weak in their faith. They don't have strong self-control yet. It is our job as "seasoned Christians" to help the new Christians grow stronger in their faith. At one point, we were all in their position.

Peter also has harsh words for those who come to Christ and then wander off into sin again. He says,

"They are worse off at the end than they were at the beginning. It would have been better for them not to have known the way of righteousness, than to have known it and then to turn their backs on the sacred."

This is really an important point. These people who come to Christ and then head back into the realm of sin are like dogs that vomit, walk away for a while, then return to their vomit to eat it.

What can we say, dear sisters and brothers? Peter really lays it out there without much filtering in 2 Peter chapter 2. What are the lessons for us? I think there are a few things we need to walk away with:

1. Sin has been with us since God created the heavens and the earth. It is still with us. We just tend not to recognize it. Let us always remember to call sin "sin." When we start defending sin, or try to explain it away, we are working against the laws of God.

2. I think another key lesson in this text is that while God has a merciful side, he is also a God of justice. God will leave no sin unpunished. I think we all need to reconcile ourselves with the fact that when we sin, we must expect consequences. And those consequences come from God because God is a God of justice. God will punish us for our rebel-

lion, just like a good parent should do. We must correct our children, and discipline them. God does the same.

3. The big picture here in today's text is that we need to be on the lookout for sinful teachers. We need to be sensitive to the reality of sin in the world. And we need to be aware that the taint of sin can even reach religious teachers. Sin can permeate the church this way. And we must be very careful to choose our pastors, shepherds, preachers, teachers, and deacons carefully. Because good leaders can be a great gift from God. But godless, corrupt leaders can lead all of our souls away from God and potentially into hell.

Let us all be sensitive to the sin around us, but fortify ourselves in the truths of God's Word so that we have a strong defense when Satan comes our way.

13. The Last Days
(2 Peter 3)

The final chapter of this book is on 2 Peter, chapter 3. It is a chapter that is often called "The Day of the Lord" in the subheadings of our Bibles. And it is so fitting that Peter ends his two epistles by talking about the last days. This is a natural topic for Peter to end on. Much like the book of Revelation is the final book of the Bible, people want to find out what is happening at the end of days. We are all curious. Christians have been curious about this topic since Bible times. And we are *still* curious about how this earth will come to an end.

Now, the most likely scenario is that you and I will die like all humans do. However, that does not mean that we will miss the last days. No, all people will be present for the last days, as the Bible teaches repeatedly that the dead in Christ shall rise, and then these events described by the apostle Peter will transpire.

Don't allow these ideas to scare you. If you walk with Christ, if you pray to him, and live your life "in Christ," then you are doing precisely what Jesus has asked you to do. Those who choose to persist in their wicked ways should be shaking in their boots, however.

Those of us who are believers in Jesus will run to Him on that last day when He comes back. We will rush to His arms, and rejoice that our beloved Lord has come back to receive us into His Kingdom. Those who do not believe, those who scoff, and those who persist in their sinfulness ... they will be fearful, for the day of the Lord will be terrible for them. They, too, will have to stand before the throne of God to be judged. Those of us who are "in Christ," however, will have no fears because since we confessed Jesus in life, then he will confess our name before God on judgment day. Jesus explains this in Luke 12:8-10,

> *8 I tell you, whoever publicly acknowledges me before others, the Son of Man will also acknowledge before the angels of God. 9 But whoever disowns me before others will be disowned before the angels of God. 10 And everyone who speaks a word against the Son of Man will be forgiven, but anyone who blasphemes against the Holy Spirit will not be forgiven.*

Similar, the apostle Paul tells us that on the last day, "Every knee will bow and every tongue will confess that Jesus is Lord of all." (Philippians 2:10-11)

So let us now turn to 2 Peter chapter 3 and see what Peter has to say to us about the last days (2 Peter 3:1-2):

> *Dear friends, this is now my second letter to you. I have written both of them as reminders to stimulate you to wholesome thinking. I want you to recall the words spoken in the past by the holy prophets and the command given by our Lord and Savior through your apostles.*

To begin this chapter, Peter points out that this is his second letter. Traditionally, we call the Petrine Epistles part of the "General Epistles" (James, 1 & 2 Peter, 1 & 2 & 3 John, and Jude). What we mean by that is that they are not written to a specific community, such as Romans was written to the Christians at Rome, and the Corinthian letters were written to the church in Corinth. First and Second Peter have a more general audience. In other words, Peter knew that when he wrote them, he was sending them to all Christians everywhere, and not specifically to one community.

Peter tells us that his purpose is to get us to have "wholesome thinking." He wants to connect us to the grand story of God's activity in the lives of human beings. He wants to connect us to the prophets of old, as well as to the teachings of Jesus our Lord, and the apostles, both of which he specifically mentions in verse 2.

In verses 3-7, Peter writes this:

> *3 Above all, you must understand that in the last days scoffers will come, scoffing and following their own evil desires. 4 They will say, "Where is this 'coming' he promised? Ever since our ancestors died, everything goes on as*

> *it has since the beginning of creation." 5 But they deliberately forget that long ago by God's word the heavens came into being and the earth was formed out of water and by water. 6 By these waters also the world of that time was deluged and destroyed. 7 By the same word the present heavens and earth are reserved for fire, being kept for the day of judgment and destruction of the ungodly.*

Peter is warning us that there are plenty of people who "scoff" at Christianity. They don't respect the Lord. They live as if there is no God. They think the whole idea of a Second Coming is ridiculous, so they mock us. They will tell us to eat, drink, and be merry, for tomorrow we die. They don't think about judgment day or eternal life. These people "deliberately" forget that there is a Creator.

These people are called atheists. They deny the existence of God. They act as if all of this just came out of nowhere. These people forget that the story of Noah is about God's wrath, and His destruction of the human race, with the exception of Noah and his family. Peter tells us here, in quite explicit terms, that fire is coming to the earth, along with a day of judgment. He then tells us that the "ungodly" will be destroyed, just like in the days of Noah. Except this time, they will be destroyed not by water, but by fire.

I honestly believe atheism is one of the most foolish positions a person can take in their thinking. It is very hard for me to conceive of all of this creation coming from nowhere. This is one of the big mysteries to the scientists: *Why do we have something rather than nothing?*

Nobody can explain it. About 3 or 4 percent of Americans are resolute atheists. However, they have no way to explain why there is something rather than nothing. If there is no God, then there should be no creation. But there is a creation. So where did it come from? Has the creation existed since eternity? That doesn't seem likely because there must be a beginning point of all things.

So, if someone wants to call us fools for believing in God, then we could argue that it is more foolish to think that all that is around us never existed, or that it had no beginning, or that everything has always been. Those ideas seem preposterous to me. I think the obvious explanation is the one that the Bible makes clear: *There is a God, and He is the Creator*. Verses 8-9 say this:

> *8 But do not forget this one thing, dear friends: With the Lord a day is like a thousand years, and a thousand years are like a day. 9 The Lord is not slow in keeping his promise, as some understand slowness. Instead, he is patient with you, not wanting anyone to perish, but everyone to come to repentance.*

Peter exhorts us to realize that the coming of Jesus might be a very long time, for a day is like a thousand years in the mind of God. This is a concept that is reinforced throughout the Bible. Psalm 90:4 says, "A thousand years in your sight are like a day that has just gone by."

In other words, some people may doubt the second coming of the Lord Jesus because it has taken a long time already. But Peter reminds us what the Old Testament clearly tells us: God doesn't care about time. He's not bound to it, as we currently are. It's all the same for God, as He exists in eternity. God is extremely patient. He gives us time to repent of our sins. He wants us to turn our lives towards Him. He wants all humankind to turn toward Him.

Now, the natural question is: Why is God taking so long? I think it is possible that God is waiting on the entire world to know His Son. Currently, about one-third of the human race claims to be Christian. My guess is that God might want to see the entire world become evangelized before the Son returns. To me, that is a real possibility. And that means that we need to be spreading the Word so that we might hasten the day of the Lord's second coming. I may be wrong here. But this seems sensible to me.

Verse 10 tells us the following:

> *The day of the Lord will come like a thief. The heavens will disappear with a roar; the elements will be destroyed by fire, and the earth and everything done in it will be laid bare.*

This passage from Peter is no surprise, as Jesus tells us the same thing. This is the concept that Jesus taught in Matthew 24:43, and it gets reiterated here in 2 Peter, in the book of Revelation (16:15), and also in 1 Thessalonians (5:2,4). In other words, Jesus will come at a time when nobody is expecting him to come. It will be a huge surprise to everyone. Let me write out those passages for you:

- Matthew 24:43, But understand this: If the owner of the house had known at what time of night the thief was coming, he would have kept watch and would not have let his house be broken into.

- Revelation 16:15, "Look, I come like a thief! Blessed is the one who stays awake and remains clothed, so as not to go naked and be shamefully exposed."

- 1 Thessalonians 5:2,4: For you know very well that the day of the Lord will come like a thief in the night. ... But you, brothers and sisters, are not in darkness so that this day should surprise you like a thief.

On that last day, there will be a loud roar in the skies, the sun and moon and all the elements will be destroyed, and then the earth and everything in it will catch fire and burn to dust, including all of the people.

Verses 11-13 tell us more about that final day:

11 Since everything will be destroyed in this way, what kind of people ought you to be? You ought to live holy and godly lives 12 as you look forward to the day of God and speed its coming. That day will bring about the destruction of the heavens by fire, and the elements will melt in the heat. 13 But in keeping with his promise, we are looking forward to a new heaven and a new earth, where righteousness dwells.

Peter then turns to how we should respond. We must "live holy and godly lives." We should actually "look forward" to that day, and hope that it comes sooner rather than later. Yes, everything will be destroyed, but God will establish "a new heaven and a new earth." It will be a "righteous" place.

Some commentators wonder if this all indicates that an asteroid will come towards earth with a roar, and will then hit the earth and burn it completely. I think that is entirely possible. The earth will meet its end through fire. Exactly *how* it happens, we do not know. But what we do know is that it will happen.

In verses 14-16, Peter says the following:

14 So then, dear friends, since you are looking forward to this, make every effort to be found spotless, blameless and at peace with him. 15 Bear in mind that our Lord's patience means salvation, just as our dear brother Paul also wrote you with the wisdom that God gave him. 16 He writes the same way in all his letters, speaking in them of these matters. His letters contain some things that are hard to understand, which ignorant and unstable people distort, as they do the other Scriptures, to their own destruction.

Peter tells us here that we don't need to fear or worry. We just need to remain at peace with Jesus, living blameless lives. We will inherit our salvation on that day.

Peter then alludes to Paul. I think this passage is a bit humorous because as we all know, Paul was an extremely cerebral academic, and his writings can be "hard to understand" as Peter readily admits. However, Paul was full of *wisdom*, according to Peter, so we should listen to Paul's teachings.

And Peter is correct that Paul talks about all of these things, for example in the Thessalonian letters. Peter then tells us that some people have distorted Paul's teachings—to their own destruction. Indeed, we need to take Paul's teachings at face value and not "distort" them. We must be very careful to allow the scriptures to speak to us directly. We must never manipulate or distort them to say what we would prefer them to say.

Finally, 2 Peter 3 closes with the following words:

> *17 Therefore, dear friends, since you have been forewarned, be on your guard so that you may not be carried away by the error of the lawless and fall from your secure position. 18 But grow in the grace and knowledge of our Lord and Savior Jesus Christ. To him be glory both now and forever! Amen.*

Peter tells us that *we have been warned*. Thus, we must stay on our guard against false teachings. We must stay firm in the faith. We must continue to grow in our knowledge of God and of Christ Jesus. That is precisely what we are called to do.

We are to "grow in grace and knowledge" of the Lord Jesus Christ.

Do not fear! Let all of this play out as it may. There's nothing you and I can do about it, since God is in control. But what we can do is to keep growing in grace, just as Peter says. And by obeying His voice, we will continue to bring glory to God. That is our Christian duty.

About the Author

If you feel generous and have a few minutes, please leave a review online where you purchased this book. It makes a significant difference to the author. Thank you in advance.

Dyron B. Daughrity is the William S. Banowsky Chair in Religion at Pepperdine University in Malibu, California. He is the author of many books and articles in the fields of comparative religion, global Christianity, and world religious history. He has ministered to churches for over 30 years, and is currently the Senior Minister at the Hilltop Community Church of Christ in El Segundo, California. Dyron has been married to Sunde for 28 years and they have four children.

Visit the author's website
https://seaver.pepperdine.edu/academics/faculty/dyron-daughrity/

Follow on social media
Facebook: https://www.facebook.com/dyron.daughrity

About the Publisher

Sulis International Press publishes select fiction and nonfiction in a variety of genres under four imprints:

- Riversong Books (fiction)
- Sulis Press (general nonfiction)
- Keledei Publications (spirituality)
- Sulis Academic Press (academic works)

For more, visit the website at
https://sulisinternational.com

Subscribe to the newsletter at
https://sulisinternational.com/subscribe/

Follow on social media
https://www.facebook.com/SulisInternational
https://twitter.com/Sulis_Intl
https://www.pinterest.com/Sulis_Intl/
https://www.instagram.com/sulis_international/

www.ingramcontent.com/pod-product-compliance
Lightning Source LLC
Chambersburg PA
CBHW032124090426
42743CB00007B/451